RISK GOVERNANCE SERIES

THE INSURANCE COMPASS

A Complete Guide to the Insurance Broker Discipline in the GCC and Middle East

DR. IBRAHIM HIKMAT KARAM

Professional Doctorate in Insurance and Risk Management

2026 PROFESSIONAL EDITION

THE RISK GOVERNANCE SERIES

Book One **The Insurance Compass**

A Complete Guide to the Insurance Broker Discipline in the GCC and Middle East

Book Two **The Insurance Constitution**

Governing Risk in a Systemic World

Book Three **Insurance Without Claims**

Redesigning Insurance Around Resilience, Not Indemnity

Book Four **Risk Ecosystem Entanglement**

A New Discipline in Insurance and Risk Management

The series begins with the practitioner. It then moves outward, from the broker, to the system, to resilience, and finally to the connected nature of risk itself.

2026 PROFESSIONAL EDITION

Cases drawn from professional practice are anonymised, adapted or, where necessary, composited from more than one file to protect confidentiality while preserving the professional issue illustrated. Public regulatory and market examples are identified as such. The analysis reflects the author's professional judgement and is offered as educational and professional reference, not legal or regulatory advice.

Regulatory position checked through 17 August 2026. Insurance regulation changes frequently. Readers should verify current requirements against the relevant regulator before relying on any jurisdiction-specific statement.

ACKNOWLEDGEMENTS

Foreword and Acknowledgements

No journey of significance is ever travelled alone. Although my name appears on the cover of this book, *The Compass* is the product of countless people whose guidance, encouragement, wisdom, patience, and support shaped both the person and the professional behind these pages.

First and foremost, I offer my deepest gratitude to my family. To my parents, whose values of integrity, perseverance, humility, and hard work became the foundation upon which my life and career were built. Their sacrifices created opportunities that I could never have achieved on my own.

To my wife and children, thank you for your unwavering love, understanding, and patience throughout the many years that this profession demanded long hours, constant travel, urgent client commitments, and moments when my attention was divided between family life and professional responsibilities. Your support has been a source of strength in every challenge and a reminder of what truly matters.

To my brother, I offer a very special and heartfelt thank you. My appreciation and love for you go far beyond what words can adequately express. You have been more than a brother; you have been a constant source of support, loyalty, encouragement, and strength throughout the different chapters of my life. Knowing that you were always there, in moments of success as well as in times of difficulty, has meant more to me than I can ever properly convey. The bond we share is one I treasure deeply, and I remain profoundly grateful for your presence in my life, your belief in me, and the unconditional brotherly love that has accompanied me throughout this journey.

To my colleagues, past and present, thank you for the lessons, the debates, the shared successes, and even the setbacks that taught us resilience. The insurance profession is fundamentally a people business, and I have been privileged to work alongside talented professionals whose commitment to clients and excellence inspired me throughout my career.

To the mentors who guided me, challenged my assumptions, and shared their knowledge with generosity, I remain profoundly grateful. Every meaningful professional achievement can be traced back to individuals who invested their time and wisdom in helping others succeed. I hope this book honours the example you set.

To the insurers, reinsurers, risk managers, regulators, clients, and industry leaders I have had the privilege of working with across the GCC and the Middle East, thank you for the trust you placed in me and for the experiences that enriched my understanding of this remarkable profession. Much of what appears in these pages has been shaped by real conversations, real challenges, and real solutions developed through decades of professional collaboration.

I am also grateful to the countless insurance professionals who often work behind the scenes without recognition. Brokers, underwriters, claims specialists, compliance officers, actuaries, and administrators play a vital role in protecting businesses, communities, and families against uncertainty. This book is dedicated to your profession and to the important work you perform every day.

Finally, I would like to thank every young professional entering the insurance industry. Your curiosity, ambition, and willingness to learn are the reasons this book was written. I hope that *The Compass* serves not only as a technical guide but also as a trusted companion throughout your professional journey.

If this book helps even one aspiring broker navigate the complexities of our profession with greater confidence, integrity, and purpose, then the effort invested in writing it will have been worthwhile.

With sincere gratitude,

Dr. Ibrahim H. Karam

"To everyone who walked into an insurance office in the Gulf without a map, without a mentor, and without a manual, and who found their way regardless. You deserved this book from the beginning."

AUTHOR'S NOTE

I did not write this book because the fundamentals of broking had changed. I wrote it because the market had.

I did not write this book because I believed the insurance profession lacked technical knowledge. The industry is full of talented people, excellent qualifications, regulatory guidance, training programmes, professional institutions and technical resources. What I felt was missing was something different. I wanted to write the book I wish had existed when I first entered the profession.

When I began my career, I learned insurance the way many professionals of my generation learned it: by doing the work. I learned from files, from claims, from policy wordings, from difficult conversations with clients, from challenging negotiations with underwriters, and from experienced professionals who were generous enough to share what they knew. Some lessons arrived through success. Many arrived through mistakes. Looking back, I realise that the profession taught me far more than any classroom ever could. It taught me how risk behaves when it leaves the pages of a textbook and enters the real world.

Over the years I noticed a recurring pattern. New entrants to the profession were often taught products but not always the profession itself. They learned how a policy worked, but not necessarily how to think like a broker. They learned how to compare quotations, but not always how to advise a client. They learned how to process a renewal, but not always how to understand a business. The profession is far deeper than policies, premiums and claims. At its best, it is a discipline built on judgement, trust, responsibility and service.
That is the reason this book exists.

I did not want to write a technical manual that would sit on a shelf and be opened only before an examination. I wanted to write something practical. Something that reflected how insurance is actually experienced by the people working in it every day. A profession is not lived through perfect frameworks and theoretical examples. It is lived through incomplete information, commercial pressure, changing regulations, difficult claims, challenging clients, market cycles, unexpected losses and decisions that must often be made before every answer is available.

Throughout my career I have had the privilege of working alongside remarkable professionals across the GCC, the Middle East and international markets. I have been fortunate to learn from supervisors, managers and business leaders whose influence on my professional development extended far beyond the organisations we worked for together. Many of my former bosses became mentors in the truest sense of the word. They challenged me when my thinking was too narrow, trusted me with responsibility before I believed I was ready, and demonstrated through their own conduct what professionalism really looked like. The lessons they shared with me, sometimes deliberately and sometimes simply by example, continue to influence the way I advise clients, lead teams and approach difficult decisions today. Their contribution to this book is far greater than they may ever realise.

My hope is that a young broker beginning their journey will find guidance, structure and direction within these chapters. I also hope that an experienced practitioner will occasionally recognise a familiar situation, pause for a moment, and perhaps see an old lesson from a slightly different perspective. If this book helps bridge the gap between technical knowledge and professional judgement, even in a small way, then it will have achieved its purpose.

Insurance remains one of the most important professions in modern society because it helps people, businesses and communities move forward despite uncertainty. It is a profession that rewards competence, integrity, curiosity and patience. It has certainly demanded all of those qualities from me over the course of my career, and it continues to do so today.

This book is written in that spirit.

Dr. Ibrahim H. Karam
Dubai, United Arab Emirates

BEFORE YOU BEGIN

You can read this book from beginning to end, but you do not have to. Part One explains the profession and market. Part Two moves through the major risk classes. Part Three is the working heart of the book: placement, relationships, negotiation and claims. Part Four deals with the pressures reshaping modern broking. The final part is about career and judgement.

The chapters are not designed to be symmetrical. Some questions need a case; others need several pages of technical explanation. A few are deliberately brief because the idea is better carried forward into practice than stretched to fill space. Read the book as a professional conversation rather than a syllabus.

When you encounter a regulatory statement, treat the date seriously. When you encounter a practice case, ask what you would have done before reading the outcome. And when you disagree with me, mark the page. Professional judgement grows faster through disagreement than through passive agreement.

CONTENTS

PART ONE

FINDING YOUR BEARINGS

The profession, the market and the rules that shape both.

CHAPTER ONE

The Broker's Real Job

I have interviewed and trained many young insurance professionals who entered broking believing that the job was mainly about finding quotations. I understand why. Quotation activity is visible. It fills inboxes, spreadsheets, comparison sheets and renewal meetings. The deeper work is harder to see. It begins before a market is approached and continues long after a policy is issued.

The broker's real job is to reduce the distance between the risk a client actually carries and the protection the client thinks it has. Sometimes that means negotiating price. Often it means saying that the cheapest quotation is not the best answer. At other times it means discovering that a risk has changed while the insurance programme has not. And when a claim arrives, it means standing beside the client with enough command of the wording, the facts and the market history to turn a promise on paper into a recovery in practice.

Over more than three decades in insurance I have learned that the strongest brokers are rarely the loudest in the room. They are the people who ask one more question before placing a risk, who read the endorsement others skim, and who can explain a difficult coverage point to a chief executive without hiding behind technical language. This chapter begins there, because everything else in this book depends on what you believe the profession is for.

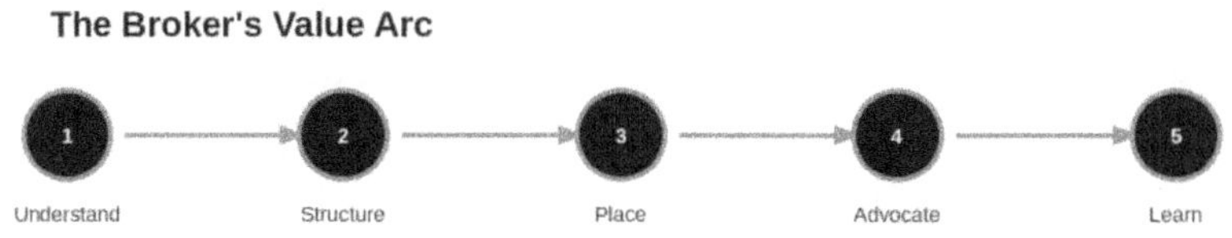

FIGURE 1 The broker creates value across the full insurance cycle, not only at placement.

1.1 The professional intermediary

An insurance broker is a licensed professional intermediary who acts on behalf of clients in the procurement, structuring, placement, and management of insurance coverage. Every element of this definition deserves careful examination, because each element distinguishes the insurance broker from other participants in the insurance market and from the common misconceptions that surround the role.

The word licensed is the first element of consequence. In every jurisdiction within the GCC and Middle East in which insurance broking is a regulated activity, a person or firm may not act as an insurance broker without holding a valid licence issued by the relevant regulatory authority. That licence is not merely a commercial permission. It is a professional credential carrying obligations to the client, to the market, and to the regulator. When a licensed broker provides advice, that advice carries the weight of the regulatory framework that licences them.

The phrase in the procurement, structuring, placement, and management of insurance coverage describes the full scope of the broker's function. It encompasses the initial assessment of the client's risk profile and coverage needs, the design of an appropriate insurance programme, the negotiation of terms with insurers, the ongoing management of the insurance relationship, and the active support of the client in the event of a claim. The broker who places a policy at inception and then disappears until the next renewal is performing the narrowest possible version of the broking function.

1.2 What the role is not

The insurance broker is not a salesperson. The broker's primary objective is to serve the client's insurance needs accurately and adequately. The broker's success is measured not by the volume of premium placed but by the quality of coverage secured, the appropriateness of that coverage to the client's actual risk profile, and the effectiveness of the advocacy provided when a claim arises. A broker who sells a client a product that pays a generous commission but does not adequately address the client's genuine risk has not succeeded commercially. They have failed professionally.

The broker is also not an insurer. The broker does not bear insurance risk. The broker does not guarantee the financial strength of the insurer whose product they place. The broker does not promise that a claim will be paid. These responsibilities rest with the insurer. Understanding the boundaries of the broker's role and responsibility is as important as understanding its scope.

The broker is not a legal adviser. Brokers in the GCC frequently encounter questions of law: coverage disputes, policy interpretation, contractual obligations. The professional broker should have a working understanding of the legal frameworks relevant to their practice. But they should not provide legal advice, and they should recommend that clients obtain independent legal counsel when legal questions are genuinely in issue.

1.3 Why the broker still matters in the Gulf

In the GCC and Middle East, the broker's value proposition has a specific and distinctive character reflecting the particular dynamics of the regional market. Three features make the broker's role especially important in this environment.

Market complexity: the regional insurance market encompasses multiple jurisdictions with significantly different regulatory frameworks, insurance cultures, and market conditions. A client with operations across the UAE, Saudi Arabia, Kuwait, and Bahrain faces a genuinely complex insurance environment. Different regulators, different minimum coverage requirements, different localisation obligations, and different documentation standards must all be navigated simultaneously.

Relationship centrality: business in the GCC and Middle East is, to a greater degree than in many Western markets, conducted on the basis of personal relationships built over time through consistent demonstration of trustworthiness and competence. The broker who has established trusted relationships with senior underwriters and senior decision-makers at client organisations can access capacity and achieve favourable terms that are not accessible through transactional approaches.

The protection gap education function: a substantial proportion of commercial clients in the regional market, particularly small and medium-sized enterprises, have a limited understanding of the insurance products available to them, the coverage they actually need, and the claims processes through which they can recover losses. The broker who educates, advises, and guides such clients is providing a service of genuine social and economic value.

1.4 Authority, mandate and responsibility

Professional indemnity insurance deserves particular mention. Most GCC jurisdictions require licensed brokers to hold professional indemnity insurance as a condition of licensing. This requirement reflects the recognition that even the most competent and diligent broker can make errors of judgement or execution that cause financial harm to clients. The broker who does not fully understand the scope of their own professional indemnity coverage is not in a position to manage the professional risk they carry.

1.5 Three tests I use for professional value

Common Professional Mistakes

1. Treating broking primarily as a sales function rather than a professional advisory discipline.
2. Creating the impression that the broker guarantees claims payment.
3. Placing cover and failing to revisit adequacy until the next renewal.
4. Presenting disclosure in a technically compliant but practically unclear way.
5. Keeping advice in memory rather than leaving a professional file trail.

The first test is the counterfactual test. Ask what would happen if the broker disappeared from the transaction. If the client would obtain the same insurer, the same wording, the same price, the same explanation and the same claims support through a direct channel, then the broker has to be honest about how much value was actually added. This is not a comfortable question, but it is useful. It forces the profession away from entitlement and toward contribution.

The second is the bad-news test. A broker who is excellent only when the market is soft has not yet been tested. What happens when the insurer refuses a requested extension, the renewal premium rises sharply, capacity withdraws, or a claim is reserved? Can the broker explain the position without blaming the market, and can they create options rather than excuses? I have learned more about colleagues in difficult renewals than in successful ones. Pressure exposes whether the relationship with the client was built on service or on favourable outcomes.

The third is the file test. Could another competent professional open the file six months later and understand why the recommendation was made? Good broking leaves a trail: the risk information received, the markets considered, the key differences in terms, the client's priorities, the reasons for the recommendation and any material limitations explained. Documentation is not bureaucracy added to advice. It is the memory of advice after people forget the conversation.

These tests also protect the broker. A market that increasingly measures conduct, complaints and customer outcomes will be less tolerant of advice that exists only as recollection. The professional file should show judgement without reading like litigation was expected from the beginning. The balance is possible: write what mattered, not everything that happened.

The point to carry forward is simple. The broker's value does not begin with access to insurers and it does not end with a policy schedule. It lives in judgement. If you build that judgement carefully, market access becomes more valuable. Without it, access is merely distribution.

CHAPTER TWO

How the Gulf Insurance Market Became What It Is

Markets leave fingerprints on the professions that grow inside them. The Gulf insurance market was shaped by trade, hydrocarbons, construction, expatriate labour, family enterprise, state-led development and, increasingly, technology. It therefore did not develop as a smaller copy of London or continental Europe. A practitioner who knows the product but not the market's history can misunderstand why today's arrangements look the way they do.

I do not offer this chapter as a museum tour. History matters because it explains present behaviour: why international capacity remains important in complex risks, why Islamic approaches to risk sharing developed alongside conventional insurance, why personal relationships still carry commercial weight, and why regulatory institutions across the region have matured at different speeds.

2.1 Risk sharing before modern insurance

Long before modern insurance companies existed, merchants and communities used partnerships, mutual support and shared responsibility to manage the consequences of uncertain trade. Islamic commercial jurisprudence also developed a sophisticated vocabulary around uncertainty, obligation and permissible risk taking. Those traditions are part of the intellectual background to modern takaful, but they should not be collapsed into a claim that medieval arrangements were insurance policies in today's legal sense.

Classical concepts such as aqilah, collective responsibility for certain financial consequences, are often discussed as historical antecedents of mutual risk sharing. Modern takaful draws more directly on structured participant contributions, tabarru and defined operator models developed under contemporary law and Sharia governance. The distinction matters academically and practically. History can illuminate a product without turning the product into something older than it really is.

2.2 Oil, trade and the arrival of modern capacity

The decisive modern transformation came with the Gulf's integration into global energy, shipping, aviation and construction markets during the twentieth century. Bahrain's commercial oil discovery in 1932 was an early milestone. Saudi Arabia and Kuwait followed in the late 1930s, while Abu Dhabi, Dubai and Oman developed their hydrocarbon industries later. Oman began commercial oil exports in 1967.

The insurance consequence was larger than oil itself. Ports expanded. Contractors arrived. Aircraft fleets grew. Industrial plants, pipelines, storage terminals and new cities created concentrations of value that required international underwriting and reinsurance capacity. Local insurers developed alongside that demand, while London and other international markets remained important for complex and high-severity risks.

2.3 The broker becomes a profession

As clients became larger and their programmes more complicated, simply introducing a buyer to an insurer was no longer enough. Independent broking grew because businesses needed someone to translate operations into underwriting information, compare competing markets, coordinate local and international capacity, and stay involved when the policy was tested by a claim.

The profession that emerged was unusually international. Gulf nationals, Arab professionals, expatriate specialists and global broking houses worked inside the same market. Formal qualifications helped professionalise that community, but much of the real craft was still learned by sitting beside experienced brokers and underwriters, reading wordings, handling claims and discovering which details mattered only after somebody had missed them once.

I recognise that apprenticeship model because it shaped my own career. The best mentors did not merely tell me what policy to buy. They taught me how to ask a client a second question, how to read an underwriter's hesitation, how to document a difficult recommendation and how to remain useful after the premium had been paid. Those lessons are harder to standardise than an examination syllabus, but they are the reason professional broking became more than distribution.

2.4 Takaful and cooperative insurance

Takaful is not a decorative regional variation. It is a distinct family of Sharia-compliant risk-sharing arrangements built around participant contributions and governance structures that separate the participants' fund from the operator's role. Modern institutional takaful developed in the late 1970s, including the Islamic Insurance Company of Sudan established in 1979, and then expanded across the Gulf and wider Muslim markets.

The practical mistake is to assume that every product described as cooperative, Islamic or takaful has the same legal architecture. It does not. Operator models, surplus treatment, Sharia oversight, accounting and regulation differ by jurisdiction. Saudi Arabia's statutory cooperative insurance model is especially important and deserves to be understood on its own terms rather than treated as a synonym for every form of takaful.

2.5 The market by 2026

The regional market is now characterised less by a single growth story than by several different ones happening at once. Saudi Arabia has a unified Insurance Authority and an explicit sector-development agenda. The UAE has strengthened broker regulation and extended mandatory worker health insurance across all emirates. Egypt is implementing a unified insurance law. Kuwait's dedicated Insurance Regulatory Unit continues to issue detailed market rules. Oman operates under the Financial Services Authority, and Jordan's central bank has supervised insurance since 2021. The common theme is institutional maturation.

For brokers, the practical implication is that technical competence now includes regulatory change management. A professional who learned the market ten years ago and stopped updating their understanding is not experienced; they are out of date.

2.6 Cooperative insurance is not a synonym for every form of takaful

One point deserves precision because regional insurance writing often blurs it. Saudi Arabia operates under a statutory cooperative insurance framework. That should not simply be described as identical to the takaful models used elsewhere. Cooperative insurance in the Kingdom has its own legal and regulatory architecture. Takaful, meanwhile, is a broader family of Sharia-compliant risk-sharing structures with different operating models, governance arrangements and accounting treatments across jurisdictions.

For a broker the distinction is practical. Product names that sound similar can carry different governance, surplus and contractual features. The safe professional habit is to understand the local structure actually being used instead of translating it into a familiar label from another market.

2.7 Why regional history still affects negotiation

The region's insurance market grew quickly alongside infrastructure and international trade. That produced a professional culture in which local relationships and international capacity developed together rather than sequentially. A broker may be negotiating with a UAE insurer whose reinsurance programme depends on global markets, a Saudi insurer operating under local cooperative rules, and a London specialist that sees the risk only through a submission. The same client can therefore be represented in several commercial languages at once.

That is one reason regional broking rewards professionals who can translate. They translate the client's operations into underwriting information, local regulation into programme requirements, and international market expectations back into a form the client can use. This translation role is more durable than simple market access.

CHAPTER THREE

Regulation in Motion

The regulatory chapter in an insurance book ages faster than almost anything else. That is why I have dated this discussion to August 2026 and deliberately avoided pretending that a printed page can replace a regulator's current rulebook. The principle is straightforward: know the architecture, know where to verify, and never rely on memory when a licence, client right or reporting obligation is at stake.

3.1 Regulation is part of the service

A broker's regulatory knowledge is not a back-office speciality. It shapes how clients are onboarded, how advice is documented, how premiums move, how complaints are handled, how conflicts are managed, and sometimes whether the broker is legally allowed to touch the transaction at all. The best commercial professionals I know do not treat compliance as something that happens after the deal. They understand enough of the framework to structure the deal correctly in the first place.

The direction of travel across the region is clear even though the rules are not uniform. Supervisors are asking for stronger governance, better evidence, clearer customer treatment, more formal risk management and more reliable reporting. Digital distribution and data use are bringing technology inside the supervisory perimeter rather than leaving it as an operational matter.

3.2 United Arab Emirates: a new brokerage operating model

The UAE mainland insurance sector is supervised by the Central Bank of the UAE. The most important recent change for brokers is the Insurance Brokers' Regulation C 1/2024, effective from 15 February 2025. It is not a minor update to an old licensing rule. It changes daily operating practice.

The Regulation requires brokers to act honestly, fairly and transparently and, when comparing products and insurers, to act in the client's best interests. It requires written client authorisation and demands that recommendations be consistent with the client's demands and needs. It also strengthens governance, financial soundness, internal control and reporting expectations.

The operational change practitioners feel most immediately is the treatment of money. For primary insurance, premiums must be paid directly by the client to the insurance company. Brokers are prohibited from collecting them. Claim settlements and premium refunds likewise move directly between insurer and client. That may sound like an accounting detail. It is actually a redesign of the cash flow, control environment and client communication process of a brokerage.

The UAE is still not one regulatory space for every insurance activity. The Dubai International Financial Centre is supervised by the Dubai Financial Services Authority. The Abu Dhabi Global Market has its own Financial Services Regulatory Authority. DIFC insurance firms can carry out authorised insurance and reinsurance activities under the DFSA framework, but federal law constrains the writing of UAE-situated risks from the centre. The practical lesson is to identify the regulatory perimeter before assuming that a licence in one part of the UAE travels with the transaction.

3.3 Saudi Arabia: consolidation, growth and enforcement

Saudi Arabia's Insurance Authority began operations in November 2023. Health insurance responsibilities transferred from the Council of Health Insurance to the Authority in March 2024, completing the move toward a unified insurance supervisor. The Authority's mandate combines regulation with development of the sector, which makes Saudi Arabia one of the region's most important laboratories for how supervision and market growth can move together.

The market continues to develop quickly. By August 2026 the Authority's public reporting page included the 2024 annual market report and quarterly sector publications through 2025, alongside a growing body of rules on motor, health, insurtech and specialised products. Enforcement is not theoretical. The Authority reported more than 2,000 supervisory and regulatory violations identified during 2025 and financial penalties of roughly SAR 25 million, alongside product suspensions for certain insurers. For a practitioner, the message is clear: rapid market growth is being accompanied by visible supervisory intervention.

Saudi insurance remains built on the cooperative insurance model. The professional mistake is to reduce that statement to terminology. Product governance, surplus arrangements, Sharia considerations where relevant, actuarial pricing, mandatory cover and customer protection all influence how the market functions. A cross-border broker needs local expertise rather than importing assumptions from another Gulf jurisdiction.

3.4 The rest of the GCC: similar direction, different institutions

Bahrain's insurance sector remains under the Central Bank of Bahrain, whose Volume 3 rulebook governs insurance and whose recent supervisory work has included claims handling, capital and market conduct initiatives. Qatar Central Bank directly supervises insurance companies and auxiliary insurance services onshore under Law No. 13 of 2012 and its insurance instructions, while the Qatar Financial Centre operates its separate framework.

Kuwait's Insurance Regulatory Unit was established under Law No. 125 of 2019 and remains the dedicated insurance supervisor. It has continued to issue implementing decisions and circulars, including a 2026 move prohibiting cash transactions across insurance policies. Oman should not be described, as older material sometimes does, as an insurance sector supervised by the Central Bank. Insurance falls under the Financial Services Authority, which regulates insurance alongside capital markets and other financial professions.

These differences matter because clients experience the region as one commercial geography while supervisors do not. A group operating in Dubai, Riyadh, Doha and Muscat may want one insurance strategy. The broker's job is to create that strategic coherence without pretending that one regulatory answer applies everywhere.

3.5 Beyond the GCC

Jordan's insurance sector has been under the Central Bank of Jordan since June 2021. Egypt's Financial Regulatory Authority now supervises the market under the Unified Insurance Law No. 155 of 2024, a significant legislative reset that also supports digital insurance distribution and stronger governance. Lebanon's Insurance Control Commission, under the Ministry of Economy and

Trade, was reactivated with new leadership appointments in 2025, and 2026 measures have continued to address intermediary financial strength and market discipline.

I mention these markets because regional careers and clients do not stop at GCC borders. The profession is mobile. So are programmes, ownership structures and claims.

3.6 From my own supervision file

In 2025 our own brokerage went through a targeted examination of its targeted financial sanctions framework by the CBUAE. The final report identified three medium-risk findings. None was a dramatic allegation of misconduct. The findings were more instructive than that: the sanctions risk assessment needed to be formally documented, the risk appetite statement required greater specificity, and screening system settings and data requirements needed stronger control and evidence.

We remediated the points by formalising the risk assessment, strengthening the risk appetite statement, locking and documenting screening parameters, enforcing key data fields and improving the evidence trail. The experience changed the way I explain compliance to commercial teams. Regulators cannot supervise good intentions. They supervise systems, decisions and evidence. If a control exists only in the head of an experienced employee, it does not yet exist at the standard a modern regulator expects.

3.7 A practical habit

Whenever I enter a new jurisdiction, I keep three questions separate. Who regulates the entity? Who regulates the product or activity? And what rule governs the transaction I am actually trying to complete? Those questions sound basic. They prevent a surprising number of expensive mistakes.

3.8 The regulatory file is part of the client file

The most useful regulatory discipline I can recommend is simple: stop treating regulation as a separate binder. The rule that affects a transaction should appear in the transaction. If a client mandate is required, the file should contain it. If a recommendation has to reflect demands and needs, the recommendation note should show the reasoning. If premiums must move directly to an insurer, the client communication and accounting workflow should make that route visible. Compliance becomes stronger when the business process itself produces the evidence.

This matters particularly in the UAE after the 2025 implementation of the new brokerage regulation. A broker can no longer rely on an old operating habit merely because it was accepted for years. The premium flow rule is a good example. It changed not only finance but the timing of cover, client reminders, credit conversations and the way insurers and brokers reconcile accounts. Regulatory change becomes operational change once it reaches a client file.

There is a second lesson. Regulators increasingly examine the quality of governance rather than the existence of policies. A beautifully written policy that staff do not follow is weaker than a modest procedure that can be evidenced from actual files. When I went through a targeted supervisory examination in the UAE, that distinction became very real. The questions eventually arrive at configuration, ownership, thresholds, escalation, training and evidence. The document is only the beginning.

For young professionals, regulation can seem like a body of rules to memorise. For senior professionals, it should become a way of thinking about authority. Who is permitted to do what? What must be disclosed? Where can money move? What evidence must remain after the transaction? Those questions are commercial questions because the answer shapes how the brokerage can operate.

3.9 A regional broker needs a verification habit

Many brokers create avoidable regulatory exposure by repeating the same habits:

1. Assuming that a licence issued in one Gulf jurisdiction automatically permits activity in another.
2. Treating the UAE as a single regulatory environment rather than recognising the different regulatory perimeters that may apply.
3. Relying on memory, precedent or market practice instead of checking the current primary regulatory source.
4. Failing to convert regulatory changes into practical operating procedures and controls.

5. Keeping compliance documentation separate from the transaction file, making it difficult to demonstrate evidence during audits or regulatory reviews.

I keep a simple mental rule: whenever a statement contains the words 'must', 'may not', 'minimum', 'licensed', 'mandatory' or a precise deadline, I want the primary source. Market custom is useful for understanding how business is done. It is a poor substitute for the rulebook when the point is regulatory.

This is especially important across the GCC because changes do not occur simultaneously. Saudi Arabia can amend a motor rule while the UAE changes broker conduct requirements and Kuwait issues a new market circular. A regional client sees one insurance programme. The broker sees several legal systems moving on different calendars. That is why professional competence now includes knowing how to verify, not simply knowing the answer from memory.

CHAPTER FOUR

The Contract Before the Claim

Insurance law is often taught as a list of doctrines. In practice, clients never call to ask about a doctrine. They call because a warehouse burned, a project is late, a third party has sued them, an insurer has reserved rights, or a loss adjuster wants information they do not understand.

The professional value of legal principles is therefore not memorisation. It is disciplined reasoning. Indemnity, insurable interest, disclosure, causation, subrogation and contribution help a broker ask the right questions, but their legal effect is not identical across every GCC jurisdiction. Statutes, civil codes, policy wording, mandatory forms and local court practice matter. I have rewritten this chapter around that distinction: principles are a compass for analysis, not a substitute for jurisdiction-specific legal advice.

4.1 Principles, wording and local law

The foundational doctrines of insurance law are taught in professional examinations and then frequently treated by practitioners as abstract legal concepts with limited day-to-day relevance. This is a mistake. These doctrines are the framework within which every policy wording is drafted, every coverage question is analysed, every claims dispute is argued, and every arbitration decision in an insurance matter is made. The broker who does not understand them will regularly encounter situations that they cannot explain to their client, cannot analyse for themselves, and cannot effectively address through professional advocacy.

4.2 Indemnity and the problem of value

The principle of indemnity holds that insurance should restore the insured to the financial position they occupied immediately before the loss, and should not place the insured in a better financial position than they would have been in had the loss not occurred. Insurance is a mechanism for financial restoration, not financial gain from loss events.

The indemnity principle explains why the average clause applies to reduce claims payments when the sum insured is less than the full value of the subject matter at risk. It explains why a property claim settlement reflects the asset's value at the time of loss rather than its original purchase price. And it sets the boundary against which claims management practices must be measured in both directions: over-settlement (enrichment of the insured) and under-settlement (systematic denial of legitimate recovery) both represent failures of the indemnity standard.

Regional Case Study

The Riyadh Warehouse: Under-Insurance and the Average Clause

A Saudi trading company insured its warehouse contents for SAR 3.5 million at policy inception. Over three years of business growth, the actual replacement value of the contents reached SAR 6 million, but the sum insured was never updated. A fire damaged contents worth SAR 2 million. The insurer applied the average clause. The settlement was calculated as 3.5 divided by 6.0, multiplied by 2 million, producing a payment of SAR 1.17 million against an actual loss of SAR 2 million. The client bore the shortfall of SAR 830,000 as a consequence of underinsurance the broker had not identified or corrected at renewal. The practical point: The broker has an ongoing professional obligation to review adequacy of sums insured at each renewal and after any material change in the client's operations or asset values. The average clause and its consequences must be explained clearly to every commercial client insuring property on a fixed sum insured basis.

4.3 Insurable interest in complex structures

In simple retail insurance, insurable interest is uncontroversial. In complex commercial structures, captives, fronting arrangements, project insurance, and joint venture programmes, the alignment between formal insurance relationship and genuine economic exposure may not be self-evident. The broker placing coverage for a joint venture in an Abu Dhabi infrastructure project must verify that every party named in the policy has a genuine and legally recognised interest in the insured subject matter at the time of placement.

The UAE Joint Venture and the Insurable Interest Question. A major infrastructure project in Abu Dhabi was executed through a joint venture between a UAE conglomerate and an international contractor. The project insurance programme, structured as a combined contractor's all risks and third-party liability placement, named both joint venture partners as insureds. During construction, the UAE conglomerate's equity interest in the joint venture was novated to a holding entity incorporated in a different jurisdiction.

The insurer's claims assessor queried whether the original named insured retained insurable interest in the project following the novation. The policy had not been endorsed to reflect the changed legal structure. What I would carry forward: Corporate restructuring during a project's construction period must trigger an immediate review of the insurance programme to ensure that insurable interest is maintained and documented for all named insureds. Failure to update the programme creates a coverage validity risk that can surface precisely when it matters most, at the point of a major claim.

4.4 Disclosure and fair presentation

Disclosure remains central to underwriting, but the legal formulation of the duty is jurisdiction-specific. English-law ideas about utmost good faith and fair presentation remain influential in international wordings and market practice, yet a broker should not assume that the same doctrine, remedy or test applies identically under every Gulf civil code or mandatory policy form. The safer professional standard is higher than the minimum legal debate: disclose material risk information accurately, answer questions honestly, document what was provided, and seek legal advice when a coverage dispute turns on local law.

The Bahrain Manufacturer: When the Question Is Narrower Than the Risk. A manufacturing client was asked on a proposal form to list claims during the previous five years. An older but significant fire sat outside that period. The narrow answer could therefore have been technically complete while still leaving the underwriter with an incomplete picture of the risk history. The broker chose to disclose the older event separately, explain the corrective work that followed and retain evidence of the discussion. The insurer was then able to price the risk with the history visible rather than discover it during a later claim. What I would take from it: proposal questions set an important minimum, but the broker should also ask whether information outside the literal box is relevant enough to create a future argument if it is left unsaid. The legal duty of disclosure varies by jurisdiction and wording. The professional habit should be consistent: when in doubt about material risk information, raise it, document it and obtain legal advice where the legal obligation itself is uncertain.

4.5 Causation when several things go wrong

The doctrine of proximate cause holds that the insurer is liable for losses caused by a covered peril, and that the relevant cause is the dominant or most effective cause in the chain of events rather than the most remote or most immediate. The proximate cause doctrine provides the analytical framework for determining which policy responds to a loss caused by multiple contributing factors.

The Kuwait Flood and the Fire That Followed. A commercial property in Kuwait suffered significant damage during a severe rainfall event. The property's electrical systems, submerged by floodwater, short-circuited and caused a fire that destroyed a substantial portion of the building's interior. The property policy covered fire but excluded flood. The insurer argued that the proximate cause of the loss was the flood, which was excluded, and that the fire was merely the mechanism through which the flood damage manifested. The insured argued that the fire was the proximate cause and should be covered regardless of what triggered the electrical failure. Why it matters: Proximate cause analysis is a tool the broker must be able to apply before a claim arises, not only in response to one. When designing a property programme, the broker should identify the compound peril scenarios most likely to be encountered in the client's specific location and ensure that the coverage programme addresses them explicitly, either through all-risks wording or through specific peril extensions.

4.6 Recovery, subrogation and overlapping cover

The doctrine of subrogation entitles the insurer, having indemnified the insured, to step into the insured's position and pursue any available recovery from third parties whose actions caused or contributed to the loss. The doctrine of contribution applies where two or more insurance policies cover the same risk, requiring that the cost of the loss be shared between the responding policies in proportion to their respective liabilities.

The Dubai Construction Subrogation. A main contractor's all risks policy responded to significant damage caused to a completed section of works by a subcontractor's negligent hot work. The insurer indemnified the main contractor and then exercised its right of subrogation, pursuing recovery against the subcontractor through the UAE courts. The subcontractor had its own public liability insurance. However, the main contractor's contract with the subcontractor contained a mutual waiver of subrogation clause. The insurer's subrogation action was therefore blocked by the contractual arrangement, an arrangement the main contractor's broker had not reflected in the insurance programme through the required waiver of subrogation endorsement. What mattered: Where contracts between the insured and third parties contain waiver of subrogation provisions, the insurance programme must reflect this through explicit endorsement. A broker who allows a client to operate under a contract that waives subrogation without having obtained the required endorsement has created a potential professional liability.

4.7 Wording is where imported practice meets local law

Gulf commercial programmes frequently use wordings influenced by London-market practice, multinational templates or global master programmes. That creates an important professional tension. The wording may have been developed in one legal tradition while the insured risk, policy issuance and claim sit in another.

The broker should resist two opposite mistakes. The first is to assume that familiar English insurance concepts automatically produce the same legal result in every local court. The second is to abandon technical wording analysis because local law differs. Both are wrong. Wording still matters enormously, but the interaction between wording and mandatory local law may require counsel when a material dispute arises.

This becomes especially important in multinational programmes. A master policy can contain difference-in-conditions or difference-in-limits provisions while local admitted policies respond under mandatory forms. The client may experience the programme as one global arrangement, but claims are still made through contracts with different legal homes. Programme design must therefore address not only coverage intention but the mechanism by which that intention becomes enforceable recovery.

A useful habit is to separate three questions. What did the parties intend commercially? What does the policy actually say? What does applicable law allow that wording to do? Coverage analysis becomes much clearer when those questions are not collapsed into one.

4.8 The clause nobody discusses at renewal

The most expensive policy wording problem is often not the dramatic exclusion everyone negotiates. It is the ordinary condition nobody revisits because it has been in the schedule for years. Notification periods, warranties, protective safeguards, valuation bases, claims cooperation clauses, other-insurance provisions and definitions of insured entities can quietly determine the outcome of a claim.

I encourage brokers to read wordings in layers. First read the insuring clause: what promise is actually being made? Then read the definitions, because definitions change the meaning of ordinary words. Then exclusions. Then conditions and claims obligations. Finally, endorsements, because an endorsement can reverse what the base wording appeared to provide. Reading only the schedule is like reading the cover of a contract.

The discipline becomes more important when several policies connect. A construction programme may include contractors all risks, third-party liability, professional indemnity, marine cargo and delay in start-up. Each can contain a different definition of occurrence, period, deductible or insured party. The claim does not respect the boundaries between documents. A delay can begin with cargo damage, pass through construction and end in lost revenue. The broker has to understand the chain before deciding which policy is 'the relevant one'.

4.9 Underinsurance is rarely a single-year mistake

Doctrine Application Checklist

INDEMNITY: Are values, basis of settlement and average implications understood?

INSURABLE INTEREST: Are all named parties and ownership changes reflected?

DISCLOSURE: Have material facts been identified, explained and documented?

CAUSATION: Have compound peril scenarios been tested against the wording?

SUBROGATION: Do contracts contain waivers requiring endorsement?

CONTRIBUTION: Could several policies respond to the same event?

When a client discovers an average clause after a loss, the immediate question is usually why the sum insured was too low. The more useful question is how long the value had been drifting. Buildings are altered, imported machinery costs change, stock peaks become larger, and replacement can require freight, duties and professional fees that were not in the original asset register. A renewal process that merely rolls last year's values forward will eventually fail somewhere.

The broker cannot value every client's assets personally, nor should they pretend to. The professional obligation is to recognise when specialist valuation is warranted, explain the consequence of inadequate values, and create a renewal process that challenges assumptions. In my experience, clients respond better when the discussion is framed around recovery rather than compliance: 'What would it actually cost you to rebuild this operation after a total loss?' That question is far more concrete than 'Is your sum insured still correct?'

CHAPTER FIVE

The Market Behind the Policy

A policy may carry the name of one insurer, but the capacity behind it can be far more complicated. Reinsurance, co-insurance, facultative placements, international markets, fronting arrangements and internal underwriting authorities all shape what a broker can realistically achieve. The client usually sees the final page. The broker has to understand the machinery behind it.

One of the most useful habits in broking is to stop asking only, 'Who gave the cheapest price?' and ask instead, 'Who is actually taking this risk, on what terms, with what claims capability, and how much confidence do I have that the promise will still be valuable when the loss arrives?'

5.1 The market is a chain of capacity

The GCC commercial insurance market is a layered structure in which risks of different sizes, complexities, and specialties are handled by different categories of market participants using different distribution channels and placement mechanisms. Understanding this architecture is the foundation of effective commercial placement strategy.

The retail segment encompasses personal lines and smaller commercial risks: motor, household, simple commercial fire, and retail health. Competition is intense, margins are compressed, and digital distribution is increasingly prominent. The commercial segment, the core of professional broking practice, encompasses mid-market commercial risks: businesses of meaningful size with complex exposures requiring professional advice. The specialty and large risk segment encompasses the most complex, high-value risks, frequently requiring access to the international market including Lloyd's of London.

5.2 Choosing an insurer is a risk decision

The financial strength of local insurers is a critical consideration for every broker placement decision. Placing business with an insurer that subsequently fails to meet its claims obligations is one of the most damaging professional outcomes a broker can be associated with. It damages the client, who has suffered a loss and is relying on insurance proceeds to recover. It damages the broker's professional reputation. And it undermines the broader market's credibility.

Financial strength assessment should encompass: the insurer's rating from a recognised rating agency where available; the insurer's regulatory solvency position relative to minimum requirements; the insurer's claims payment history and reputation; and the quality of the insurer's reinsurance arrangements, which affect their capacity to meet large individual claims and accumulation losses.

The Muscat Contractor and the Failing Insurer. An Omani construction contractor placed its project insurance programme with a locally licensed insurer that offered significantly lower premiums than the market alternatives. The broker, under client pressure to reduce insurance costs, did not conduct a formal financial strength assessment and did not investigate the insurer's reinsurance arrangements. Eighteen months into the project, the insurer experienced severe financial difficulties driven by reserve inadequacy across its portfolio. Following a major project loss, the contractor discovered that the insurer's reinsurance recoveries were in dispute and that the insurer's own capital was insufficient to meet the claim independently. The recovery process extended over three years and produced a significantly reduced settlement. The broking lesson: Premium is not the correct basis for insurer selection. The broker who allows a client to make an insurer selection decision on price alone, without adequate assessment of financial strength, has failed in a fundamental professional obligation. The conversation about price must always be accompanied by the conversation about security.

5.3 London, DIFC and international capacity

Lloyd's of London is a marketplace, not a single insurance company. It is a regulated marketplace in which multiple underwriting syndicates, each separately capitalised, write insurance and reinsurance risks. Lloyd's remains the global leader for specialty and complex commercial risks, and its role in the GCC market, particularly for energy risks, large construction programmes, political risk, and specialty commercial coverage, remains significant.

Accessing Lloyd's requires working through a Lloyd's broker specifically authorised to place business in the market. The regional broker who needs to access Lloyd's for a client placement must do so either through their own Lloyd's broking affiliate or through a correspondent Lloyd's broker. This relationship, between the regional broker and the Lloyd's broker, must be managed professionally to ensure that the client's risk is presented accurately and that the terms obtained genuinely reflect the market's assessment of the risk.

5.4 Reinsurance: the capacity behind the capacity

Understanding reinsurance is important for the broker because the reinsurance arrangements of local insurers directly affect their capacity, pricing, and financial resilience. Local GCC insurers are net purchasers of international reinsurance capacity: they cede a significant proportion of their premium income to international reinsurers in order to manage their individual risk exposure and to access capacity for risks that exceed what their own capital allows them to retain.

This dependency on the international reinsurance market means that conditions in the global reinsurance market directly affect what is available to policyholders locally. When major reinsurers tighten their terms following significant global loss events, as occurred following major catastrophe years, local market capacity contracts and pricing increases, regardless of the loss experience of any individual GCC client.

5.5 Hard markets, soft markets and memory

Insurance markets move through cycles of varying duration and amplitude. Soft market conditions are characterised by competitive pricing, broad coverage availability, and ease of placement. Hard market conditions are characterised by limited competition, elevated pricing, restricted coverage terms, and difficulty placing certain risk categories. The broker who explains market cycles to clients proactively, helping them understand the structural causes of market movements and the appropriate strategies for managing their programmes through different phases, is providing genuinely valuable advisory service.

The technical knowledge that defines the competent professional and that clients rely upon when making consequential coverage decisions

The cheapest insurer is not always the cheapest decision. On a difficult corporate placement, the lowest quotation can be attractive enough to stop the conversation. I ask clients to look one step further: financial strength, claims capability, wording quality, local service, reinsurance support where relevant, and the insurer's willingness to engage when facts are imperfect. I have seen a small premium saving disappear many times over in claims friction. That does not mean the most expensive insurer is automatically better. It means price should be evaluated inside the quality of the promise.

5.6 Insurer selection is a portfolio decision

Financial-strength ratings matter, but they are not a complete insurer-selection method. A strong rating tells you something important about financial capacity. It tells you much less about how a particular claims team handles a construction loss, whether a medical network works for a specific workforce, how quickly endorsements are issued, or whether a complex liability notification will receive experienced attention.

Over time, a brokerage develops an evidence base that sits between formal ratings and anecdote. Claims response times, policy issuance quality, endorsement accuracy, complaints, settlement behaviour, technical appetite and responsiveness all contribute. I believe firms should use this information carefully. It should improve recommendations, not become a private blacklist based on one difficult file.

There is also concentration risk. A broker can become too dependent on one insurer because the relationship is easy, the systems connect well or the terms are usually competitive. That convenience can become a weakness if appetite changes suddenly. The client's programme deserves genuine market consideration even where the incumbent relationship is strong.

The mature question is therefore not 'which insurer do we like?' It is 'which insurer, for this risk, at this time, with this wording and service requirement, gives the client the best overall proposition?' That question is slower. It is also the question the client is paying a professional to answer.

5.7 Capacity has a personality

Two insurers can have similar ratings and very different appetites. One may understand food manufacturing but dislike combustible panels. Another may write construction aggressively but restrict design exposure. A third may have excellent property capacity but limited appetite for a difficult jurisdiction. Reinsurance arrangements, internal portfolio concentrations and recent claims can change those appetites between renewals.

A broker therefore learns markets in two ways. The formal way is through published appetite, ratings, wordings and underwriting guidelines. The informal but equally legitimate way is through repeated transactions: which questions an underwriter asks, where authority sits, how quickly the market escalates an exception, and whether a provisional indication survives internal referral. This is not about favours. It is about understanding how a market actually makes decisions.

That knowledge is valuable only if it remains client-focused. Market relationships can become a trap when familiarity turns into automatic placement. The test I use is whether I could explain to the client why this insurer is appropriate without mentioning how well I know the underwriter. If I cannot, the relationship has started to replace the analysis.

5.8 Reinsurance is invisible until it is not

Commercial Placement Quality Standard

RISK ASSESSMENT: Material exposures and changes are documented.

INSURER SECURITY: Financial strength and claims capability are assessed.

COVERAGE ADEQUACY: Gaps, exclusions, limits and conditions are explained.

MARKET OPTIONS: Relevant local and international options are considered.

DOCUMENTATION: Issued wording matches the terms agreed.

CLIENT ADVICE: The recommendation and remaining trade offs are clear.

Most clients do not need a lecture on treaty structures. They do need to understand that local capacity sometimes rests on reinsurance support, especially for large property, engineering, energy, aviation and catastrophe exposures. A local insurer can be the legal counterparty while a substantial part of the economic risk is distributed internationally.

For the broker this creates a practical responsibility. A facultative placement may require information at a level of detail that seems disproportionate to the local quote because an international reinsurer is making the real capacity decision. Late changes can then require another approval chain. The client experiences delay; the broker should understand where the delay lives.

The better response is not to complain that the market is slow. It is to anticipate the information that the final risk taker will need and build it into the submission early. Complex insurance becomes much easier when information travels once, clearly, instead of being reconstructed at every layer.

A placement is only as strong as the capacity, wording and claims behaviour behind it. Price is visible immediately. Quality usually reveals itself later.

PART TWO

READING RISK

Products matter. The deeper skill is seeing how risks connect inside a real business.

CHAPTER SIX

Reading an Insurance Programme as a Whole

Insurance is organised into lines of business because markets need categories. Clients do not live in categories. A single fire can trigger property damage, business interruption, machinery breakdown, liability, marine delay, cyber disruption and employee issues at the same time. The professional broker learns the individual lines, then learns to stop thinking in lines when advising a real business.

This chapter is intentionally shorter than the ones around it. Its purpose is to provide the map before we walk through the territory.

6.1 Why insurance has lines of business

Insurance products are organised into categories known as lines of business, which group products sharing similar risk characteristics, coverage principles, regulatory treatment, and actuarial methodology. The major commercial insurance lines relevant to GCC broking practice can be organised into five broad categories: property and casualty coverage; liability coverage in its various forms; marine and transport coverage; financial lines and specialty coverage; and life, health, and employee benefit coverage.

6.2 Where the lines collide

One of the most valuable insights that distinguishes the experienced professional from the new entrant is the understanding that lines of business do not operate in isolation. The risks faced by a commercial client rarely respect the boundaries that insurance categories impose. A fire at a manufacturing facility produces simultaneously a property loss, a business interruption loss, a liability exposure to third parties, a potential environmental liability, and possibly an employer's liability exposure if employees are injured.

The broker who designs an insurance programme must therefore think systematically about the full range of a client's exposures and the interactions between policies that may be triggered by the same underlying event. Gaps between policies, where a loss falls in the space between one policy's scope and another's, are one of the most common sources of consequential surprises for commercial clients when a claim arises.

The Abu Dhabi Food Manufacturer: The Gap Between Property and Liability. An Abu Dhabi food manufacturing company held a commercial property policy and a public liability policy. A fire in the production facility caused damage to the building and equipment (property claim), interrupted production for four months (business interruption claim), and resulted in smoke damage to neighbouring premises (third-party property damage under the public liability policy). The business interruption policy had a twelve-month indemnity period, which proved adequate. However, the third-party liability claim included losses from a neighbouring cold storage facility whose refrigeration system failed due to smoke ingress, a consequential financial loss rather than direct physical damage. The public liability policy's definition of property damage was argued by the insurer not to extend to the refrigeration failure. The broking lesson: Programme design must consider not only the direct loss scenarios for each line of business but also the consequential losses to third parties that may arise from those scenarios. Where consequential third-party financial losses are a material exposure, the liability policy wording should be reviewed specifically for its treatment of consequential loss.

6.3 Mandatory cover as part of programme design

Mandatory insurance should be mapped by jurisdiction, entity and activity rather than memorised as a regional list. Compulsory motor liability is a foundational requirement across the Gulf, but health, workers' compensation or employment injury, professional indemnity and sector-specific covers vary materially in legal basis and scope. The UAE's employment-linked health framework, for example, now extends across all emirates, while Saudi Arabia operates its own mandatory health and cooperative insurance architecture.

For a broker, the practical tool is a mandatory-cover map for each client. Where is the entity incorporated? Where do employees work? Which vehicles, premises and regulated professions are involved? What does a contract require beyond the statutory minimum? This prevents the common mistake of treating a GCC-wide programme as though one jurisdiction's compulsory rules travel with it.

6.4 The programme view

One of the fastest ways to spot an inexperienced programme is to look for the spaces between policies. A property policy may assume a contractor is responsible for certain damage. The contractor's liability policy may exclude the same contractual obligation. A cyber policy may cover incident response while the property wording treats data as non-physical. A marine policy may end when goods reach a warehouse even though the stock policy does not begin until a different contractual point.

No individual policy looks obviously wrong. The gap exists only when the programme is viewed as a system.

I use three lenses when reviewing a programme. The first is asset and activity: what can be damaged, interrupted, sued, stolen, delayed or lost? The second is contractual: what liabilities has the client accepted through leases, supply agreements, construction contracts, financing documents or service agreements? The third is dependency: which suppliers, utilities, technology platforms, people or customers could cause serious financial loss even without damage to the client's own assets?

Lines of business then become tools for answering those exposures, not boxes that define them. This change in order, exposure first and product second, is one of the most important habits a broker can learn.

6.5 Start with the balance sheet, not the product list

When I review a new corporate client, I find it more useful to ask what could damage the balance sheet than to ask which policies they already buy. Assets can be damaged. Revenue can stop. A third party can allege injury or financial loss. A key employee can die. Goods can disappear in transit. A regulator can impose a penalty. A cyber incident can stop operations. A customer can fail to pay. Each loss pathway points toward one or more insurance solutions, but the conversation begins with the business.

This also reveals self-insurance. Every programme contains retained risk through deductibles, exclusions, uninsured perils and limits. Some retention is deliberate and economically rational. Some is accidental. The broker's job is not to insure everything. It is to make the retained risk visible enough that the client can decide whether it is acceptable.

A useful programme review therefore ends with more than a list of policies. It should leave the client able to answer three questions: what could cause a serious loss, which part of that loss is transferred, and what remains with us? If the client cannot answer those questions, the programme may be comprehensive on paper and still poorly understood.

CHAPTER SEVEN

Property, Business Interruption and Engineering

Property insurance looks simple from a distance. There is a building, there is a value, and there is a fire policy. Most serious property disputes begin in the distance between those three statements and reality.

Values move. Stock accumulates. construction work begins inside occupied premises. Machinery is replaced. Business interruption dependencies stretch across suppliers and customers. A sum insured that was sensible two years ago can become dangerously inadequate without anybody consciously deciding to underinsure the business. Property broking is therefore less about insuring objects than about keeping the insurance model aligned with a living operation.

7.1 Property is a valuation problem before it is a claims problem

Property insurance covers physical loss or damage to the insured's property arising from defined perils. The standard commercial property policy in the GCC market is most commonly written on an all-risks basis, covering all causes of physical loss or damage except those specifically excluded, rather than on a named perils basis, which covers only those perils specifically listed.

The all-risks basis offers significantly broader coverage than named perils and is generally appropriate for commercial clients with complex property exposures. However, the breadth of all-risks coverage makes the exclusions critically important: the coverage is limited by everything that is excluded. Common exclusions in GCC commercial property policies include: war and terrorism (frequently offered as a separate extension); nuclear and radioactive contamination; wilful misconduct; gradual deterioration and wear and tear; corrosion; cyber-related events (increasingly introduced as an explicit exclusion); and acts of a competent governmental authority.

The GCC has specific natural hazard characteristics that significantly shape the property market. Sandstorms and dust cause significant damage to exposed equipment, vehicles, and building fabric across the Gulf. Flash flooding is an increasing concern in urban areas where rapid development has outpaced drainage infrastructure. The April 2024 rainfall event in the UAE, which caused widespread flooding in Dubai and other emirates, demonstrated the scale of property damage that can arise from events that the regional market had historically treated as low-probability.

Regional Case Study

The Dubai Flash Flood: Adequacy of Flood Coverage

After the severe April 2024 rainfall in the UAE, a commercial property owner faced a coverage discussion over water damage at ground-floor premises. The policy was written on an all-risks basis, but the relevant definitions, exclusions and endorsements still had to be read against the actual mechanism of the loss. The file quickly became a factual exercise: where had the water come from, how had it entered, what had been damaged, which wording applied and what evidence could establish the sequence? The broking lesson is not that an 'all-risks' label guarantees a flood outcome. It does not. The lesson is that peril definitions and endorsements should be tested before a catastrophe, and that during a disputed claim the broker should separate facts, wording and legal interpretation rather than promise a result the contract may not support.

7.2 Business interruption: insuring time and dependency

Business interruption insurance covers the financial losses suffered by a business as a result of a physical damage event that interrupts normal operations. It is one of the most commercially important and technically complex lines in the commercial insurance market, and it is frequently undervalued or incorrectly structured by clients who do not fully understand its mechanics.

The maximum indemnity period, the longest period for which the insurer will pay business interruption losses, is one of the most critical parameters in the policy and is frequently set too short by clients who underestimate the time required to restore full operations following major property damage. For manufacturing businesses dependent on specialist equipment with long lead times, or for businesses occupying premises that require significant reconstruction, a twelve-month indemnity period is routinely inadequate.

The Jeddah Pharmaceutical Manufacturer: The Inadequate Indemnity Period. A Jeddah-based pharmaceutical manufacturer insured its business interruption risk for a maximum indemnity period of twelve months. The company manufactured specialist drug formulations on customised production lines incorporating equipment from European suppliers with typical lead times of fourteen to eighteen months. A fire destroyed the principal production facility. Despite an excellent claims response from the insurer within the policy terms, the actual period required to restore full production capacity was twenty-two months: fourteen months for equipment manufacture and delivery, and eight months for regulatory recertification of the facility under Saudi Food and Drug Authority requirements. The business bore uninsured interruption losses for the final ten months of the recovery period. What mattered: Business interruption indemnity period advice requires genuine analysis of the client's specific supply chain, equipment lead times, and regulatory recertification requirements, not application of a market standard that may be entirely inadequate for the client's circumstances. The broker should document the analysis and the client's instruction on indemnity period selection in the placement file.

7.3 Engineering cover and changing physical risk

Engineering insurance is one of the most commercially significant lines in the GCC market, reflecting the region's position as host of some of the world's most ambitious construction and infrastructure projects. Contractors All Risks (CAR) insurance covers physical loss or damage to a construction project during the construction period, typically covering the permanent works, the contractor's plant and equipment, and third-party liability arising from construction operations. Erection All Risks (EAR) provides similar coverage for the installation of mechanical and electrical plant. Machinery Breakdown covers sudden and unforeseen physical damage to machinery in operation.

The GCC construction environment has specific risk characteristics: extreme summer heat creates challenges for concrete curing and increases equipment failure rates; sabkha soil conditions in coastal areas create foundation risks; dust and sand ingestion creates specific hazards for mechanical and electrical equipment. The broker advising on engineering insurance in the GCC must understand these hazards and ensure they are addressed in the coverage programme.

The Doha Metro Project: Deductible Aggregation in a Major Programme. A major infrastructure programme in Qatar involved a complex CAR insurance structure covering multiple simultaneous construction packages over an extended period. The programme incorporated a standard each-and-every-loss deductible for property damage and separate deductibles for third-party liability. During a period of intensive construction activity, a single event causing damage to the permanent works of two separate but physically adjacent packages was treated by the insurer as two separate occurrences, each attracting its own deductible, rather than as a single occurrence with one deductible. The contractual basis for this position was ambiguous in the policy wording. The broking lesson: In complex multi-package construction programmes, the deductible structure and the definition of occurrence must be negotiated explicitly at placement. The broker should ensure that the policy wording addresses clearly whether damage affecting multiple packages simultaneously constitutes one or multiple occurrences for deductible purposes.

7.4 Valuation drift is a governance problem

Inflation, imported equipment costs, construction inflation, currency movement and rapid business growth can make yesterday's values wrong without any dramatic event. This is particularly important in Gulf markets where replacement equipment may be imported and reinstatement can depend on specialist contractors and long lead times. A renewal process that copies last year's values and applies a percentage uplift is often too crude for large risks.

7.5 The April 2024 UAE floods changed a familiar conversation

The severe rainfall and flooding that affected the UAE in April 2024 gave many policyholders a practical lesson in something brokers had discussed for years: peril definitions, deductibles, drainage, basement exposure, stock location and business interruption assumptions matter most when an event is no longer hypothetical.

The professional lesson is not to overreact by assuming that every flood exposure requires the same solution. It is to stop treating flood as a tick-box extension. Where is the property? Is critical equipment below grade? What is the elevation of stock? Are there flood barriers or drainage vulnerabilities? Can staff reach the site after a major event? Is access prevention covered? Does the business interruption wording respond only after insured physical damage, or are there relevant extensions?

Business interruption deserves equal attention. A factory can repair physical damage in six weeks and still take six months to restore customer volume. A hotel can reopen while part of its destination remains disrupted. A distributor can have undamaged stock and no way to move it. The indemnity period is therefore a judgement about recovery, not repair.

When I review an indemnity period, I ask the client to describe the recovery sequence in operational language. How long to assess the loss? To obtain permits? To order replacement machinery? To ship it? To reinstall and test? To rebuild stock? To regain customers? The sum of those stages is often longer than the period chosen on the old policy schedule.

7.6 Business interruption is where operational knowledge becomes insurance knowledge

The hardest part of business interruption is rarely the formula. It is understanding how the business actually earns money. A manufacturer may depend on one imported production line. A distributor may be more exposed to warehouse access than to building damage. A hotel may reopen physically while bookings remain depressed. A data centre may have redundant equipment but a single external power dependency. The policy cannot be designed well until the operational bottleneck is known.

I ask clients to imagine a serious but plausible loss and walk through the recovery week by week. What stops immediately? Which costs continue? What can be outsourced? Which customers can wait? How quickly can equipment be replaced? Is there a temporary location? Which approvals or certifications delay restart? Somewhere in that conversation the indemnity period stops being an arbitrary number and becomes a recovery assumption.

The same exercise often reveals contingent exposures. A client's own premises may be resilient while a sole supplier is not. A business may have several customers but one customer represents forty per cent of revenue. Utility failure, denial of access and supplier or customer extensions can therefore matter more than another minor property extension. These are not automatically covered and they should not be assumed.

The professional standard is not to predict the exact loss. It is to make the recovery logic explicit before a loss tests it.

7.7 Engineering cover follows change

Common mistakes include Rolling forward property values without testing reinstatement cost; Using a twelve month indemnity period as a default rather than a recovery assessment; Treating flood as a tick box extension without testing definitions and exposures; Ignoring handover points between construction, testing and operational cover; Failing to examine deductible aggregation in complex projects.

Engineering risks are dynamic by nature. Machinery is installed, tested, maintained, modified and sometimes operated beyond the conditions that existed when it was insured. Construction sites change every week. A risk survey is a snapshot of something that refuses to stay still.

That is why handover points matter. A project can move from construction to testing, from testing to operational use, and from contractor control to owner control. Insurance arrangements need to move with it. Gaps often appear at interfaces: temporary works remain on site, completed sections are occupied, defects periods begin, or equipment arrives before the permanent property programme is ready.

The broker who understands those transitions can ask better questions at the right time. The policy should follow the risk, not the calendar date printed on the renewal diary.

> *Property losses are rarely caused by a spreadsheet error, but the size of the uninsured loss often is.*

CHAPTER EIGHT

Liability and Financial Lines

Liability insurance is different from property insurance in one important respect: the loss often begins with an allegation rather than visible damage. A letter from a lawyer can create an event before anyone knows whether the allegation is justified. That changes the broker's work. Notification discipline, defence costs, jurisdiction, wording interpretation and the relationship between contractual obligations and policy coverage become central.

In the Gulf, that complexity is amplified by multinational contracts, different legal systems, professional services, construction obligations, directors' duties and rapidly evolving cyber and data exposures. The product names are familiar. The real work lies in the wording.

8.1 Liability begins with responsibility

Liability insurance covers the legal obligation of the insured to compensate third parties who have suffered loss, injury, or damage as a consequence of the insured's acts, omissions, products, or operations. The liability insurance environment in the GCC has several distinctive characteristics arising from the specific legal frameworks of the region, the cultural context of dispute resolution, and the regulatory requirements applicable to liability coverage.

8.2 Bodily injury, local law and limit selection

Bodily-injury and death claims require particular care because liability can be shaped by mandatory local law, court practice, statutory rules, policy forms and, in some jurisdictions and circumstances, concepts such as diya or blood money. A regional broker should not reduce those influences to a single GCC-wide formula. The legal basis, recoverable heads of loss and compulsory limits must be checked in the jurisdiction where the exposure sits.

For programme design, the more useful question is severity. How many people could be injured in one event? What contractual liabilities has the client accepted? Are defence costs inside or outside the limit? Are employees, passengers, subcontractors or members of the public exposed? Where the answer depends on legal quantification, local counsel should be involved. A familiar regional term is not a substitute for current law.

The Saudi Fleet: When Compulsory Cover Is Not the Whole Programme. A Saudi logistics fleet suffered a severe multi-vehicle accident involving serious bodily injury. The immediate focus was the compulsory motor policy, but the wider discussion exposed a familiar planning problem: the client had treated statutory cover as though it were a complete assessment of liability severity. The event required the broker and local advisers to examine the policy limit, the applicable compensation framework, the company's contractual responsibilities and whether any additional liability protection could respond. Why it matters: compulsory insurance establishes a legal floor, not a universal risk appetite. Fleet clients should understand the current local policy form and test realistic severe-loss scenarios with their broker and, where legal quantification matters, local counsel. The precise compensation rules and available extensions must be verified in the jurisdiction rather than assumed from regional custom.

8.3 Public liability, professional indemnity and D&O

Public liability insurance covers the insured's legal liability to members of the public who suffer bodily injury or property damage as a result of the insured's business operations. It is a fundamental coverage for any business with a physical presence or operations that create exposure to third-party injury or property damage, and is increasingly required as a condition of regulatory licence, tender submission, or premises occupation across the GCC.

Professional indemnity insurance covers the legal liability of professionals for the financial consequences of errors, omissions, or negligent acts in the provision of professional services. Insurance brokers are themselves required to carry professional indemnity insurance in most GCC jurisdictions as a condition of their broking licence. Directors and officers liability insurance covers the personal liability of corporate directors and officers for alleged wrongful acts in their management responsibilities. As GCC corporate governance standards have risen and regulatory enforcement has become more assertive, D&O has evolved from a peripheral specialty product to a core governance tool for well-managed organisations.

The UAE Engineering Firm: Professional Indemnity and the Design Error. A UAE-licensed engineering consultancy provided structural design services for a residential development in Dubai. A design error in the foundation specification, discovered during construction, required significant remedial works. The developer sought compensation from the engineering firm for the cost of the remedial works and the resulting construction delay. The engineering firm's professional indemnity policy covered negligent acts in the provision of professional services. However, the policy contained a project-specific aggregate limit that had been set at the time of placement based on the consultancy fee rather than the potential project damage value. The remediation and delay costs significantly exceeded the project aggregate limit. Why it matters: Professional indemnity limits for engineering and design consultancies should be assessed relative to the potential project damage value for which the professional may be liable, not relative to the professional fee. The broker advising technical professionals in the GCC must understand this distinction and ensure that limits are adequate to the client's actual liability exposure.

8.4 Liability programmes are increasingly contractual programmes

A significant part of modern liability exposure is created not by tort law alone but by contracts. Clients accept indemnities, hold-harmless clauses, liquidated damages, waivers, additional-insured obligations, fitness-for-purpose standards and insurance requirements. The broker does not replace legal counsel, but cannot responsibly design liability cover without seeing the contracts that create the exposure.

Professional indemnity illustrates the point. Two engineering firms with similar revenue can carry very different risk depending on the services they perform, the jurisdictions they serve, the contractual standard of care, use of subconsultants, project types, retroactive exposure and aggregation of claims. A premium comparison that ignores these differences is not meaningful.

Directors' and officers' liability has also become more important as regional companies institutionalise governance, raise capital, list securities, expand cross-border and face stronger regulatory expectations. D&O is often purchased by finance or legal teams, but the broker should understand the governance story behind the application: ownership, board composition, financial condition, litigation, regulatory history and transaction activity.

The recurring lesson is that liability limits should not be chosen by copying peers. The right limit is a decision about plausible severity, contractual transfer, legal environment, defence cost and balance-sheet tolerance.

8.5 Contract review is insurance work even when legal advice is not

A broker should not draft the client's commercial contract unless qualified to do so. But ignoring the contract is equally dangerous. Indemnities, limitation clauses, waivers, additional-insured requirements, insurance limits and responsibility for subcontractors can change the risk the client has agreed to carry.

The useful boundary is clear. The lawyer advises what the contract means and whether the client should accept the obligation. The broker explains whether the insurance programme is designed to support that obligation, where it does not, and what the market may or may not be willing to cover. Good advisers work beside each other rather than pretending one discipline can replace the other.

I have seen insurance specifications copied from old contracts without anyone asking whether they fit the current project. Limits can be arbitrary. Required policy names can be obsolete. Waivers can conflict with subrogation rights. A contract may demand cover that the market does not provide in the way the clause assumes. Raising that problem before signature is useful broking. Raising it after a claim is archaeology.

8.6 Financial lines require a different client conversation

D&O, professional indemnity, crime and cyber policies often protect intangible exposures. There may be no asset register that tells the broker how much cover is needed. Limit selection becomes an exercise in scenario thinking, contract size, regulatory exposure, litigation environment, balance-sheet resilience and peer practice.

The proposal process is also sensitive. A professional indemnity application may ask about circumstances that could give rise to a claim, not only reported claims. A D&O renewal can be affected by transactions, investigations, capital raising or governance events. The broker should create enough trust that the client discloses uncomfortable facts early. Surprise is rarely helpful once the insurer has bound the risk.

CHAPTER NINE

Marine, Aviation and the Geography of Trade

The Gulf was a trading region before it was an oil region. Marine insurance therefore feels less like a specialist appendix here than part of the economic bloodstream. Ports, free zones, aviation hubs and global supply chains mean that cargo, hull, liability and delay exposures cross borders constantly.

The danger for a generalist broker is to treat marine and aviation as technical islands. They are not. They connect contract law, geography, sanctions, political risk, logistics, weather, accumulation and international claims practice. Even when a specialist market leads the placement, the client-facing broker needs enough command of the subject to know what questions to ask.

9.1 Cargo, hull and contractual geography

Marine insurance has a special significance in the GCC reflecting the region's geography, its historical commercial traditions, and its position as one of the world's most trade-intensive economic zones. The GCC states are among the most import-dependent economies in the world: virtually all goods that sustain their economies arrive by sea. The Port of Jebel Ali in Dubai is among the world's busiest commercial ports by container volume, and the network of ports across the GCC handles an extraordinary range and volume of cargo.

Marine cargo insurance covers physical loss or damage to goods in transit. The Institute Cargo Clauses provide the standard coverage framework used in the vast majority of cargo placements globally. Clauses A provide all-risks equivalent coverage, the broadest option, covering all causes of physical loss or damage except those specifically excluded. Clauses B and C provide progressively narrower named-perils coverage. The broker advising a commercial client on cargo insurance must assess which clause set is appropriate for the specific goods, trade routes, packaging standards, and risk management practices of the client.

The Sharjah Re-Exporter: Clauses C and the Theft Gap. A Sharjah-based re-exporter of consumer electronics purchased marine cargo insurance on Institute Cargo Clauses C, attracted by the lower premium relative to Clauses A. Clauses C do not cover theft, pilferage, or non-delivery, risks that are highly material for electronics cargo. During a shipment through a transhipment port, a significant quantity of high-value electronics was pilfered from the cargo. The cargo insurer declined the claim on the basis that theft was not a named peril under Clauses C. The client had not understood the coverage difference between Clauses A and C, and the broker had not explained it. The practical point: The broker advising on marine cargo insurance must explain the coverage differences between Institute Cargo Clauses A, B, and C clearly and document the client's informed selection. For cargo categories with significant theft exposure, electronics, pharmaceuticals, luxury goods, and consumables, the selection of Clauses C on cost grounds alone is a professional failure of advice.

9.2 Aviation: specialist capacity and high consequence

The GCC is home to some of the world's leading airlines. Aviation hull and liability insurance for commercial carriers is specialist professional territory requiring deep technical knowledge and access to specialist markets at Lloyd's and in the company market. The commercial broker is more likely to encounter aviation risk through general aviation clients (private and business aircraft), cargo operators, aerospace manufacturing and maintenance clients, and the aviation liability programmes of airports and ground handlers. Each of these categories has distinct technical characteristics requiring specialist underwriting input.

When a marine matter becomes a legal matter. In a recent maritime matter involving a commercial dredger, the insurance issue could not be handled responsibly as an insurance file alone. External maritime counsel prepared a legal position and the broker's role became one of coordination: preserve the insurance position, make sure the factual record was complete, keep the client informed, and avoid making a legal argument that belonged to counsel. This is a useful boundary for young brokers. Advocacy does not mean pretending to be every specialist. It means knowing when another specialist must be brought into the room and then making sure the insurance consequences are not lost in the legal process.

9.3 Cargo insurance is a contract-reading discipline

Marine cargo claims frequently turn on details outside the insurance certificate: the sale contract, Incoterms, packing responsibilities, title transfer, the voyage, storage arrangements and the moment risk passed from seller to buyer. That is why cargo broking is inseparable from commercial documentation.

Institute Cargo Clauses remain the common international vocabulary, but simply writing 'ICC(A)' on a schedule does not finish the analysis. Exclusions, delay, inherent vice, packing, war, strikes, temperature control, storage and accumulation all matter. For high-value or sensitive goods, the transit story should be understood before the clause is selected.

Sanctions add another layer. A cargo may be perfectly insurable in physical-risk terms and problematic because of vessel ownership, destination, counterparties or payment channels. Brokers working with international marine markets should treat sanctions screening as part of placement discipline, not an administrative check after terms are agreed.

9.4 The voyage is a chain of custody

Marine cargo becomes easier to understand when the voyage is treated as a chain of custody rather than a line on a map. Who packs the goods? Who loads them? Where does the seller's risk end? Where does the buyer's begin? Is there intermediate storage? Are goods carried on deck? Is temperature monitored? Which documents prove condition at handover? A loss can occur at any of those transitions.

This is why Incoterms matter to insurance without being insurance terms. They allocate commercial responsibilities between buyer and seller and can determine who carries risk at a particular point. The broker should understand the sale contract well enough to know whose interest is being insured and for how long.

In the Gulf, re-export and free-zone trade add another layer. Goods may enter a warehouse, be repacked, consolidated and sent onward to a third country. A conventional warehouse-to-warehouse assumption may not describe the real journey. Storage extensions, transshipment, accumulation and sanctions screening can become central.

9.5 Marine claims reward documentation

A cargo claim can be weakened before the broker hears about it. Packaging is discarded, survey rights are lost, carriers are not put on notice, delivery receipts are signed clean despite visible damage, or salvage is disposed of prematurely. The first advice after a transit loss should therefore be operational: protect the goods, preserve evidence, notify relevant parties and avoid prejudicing recovery rights.

The broker's role is to make that protocol familiar before the emergency. A one-page cargo-claim instruction given at inception can be more valuable than a long presentation after the loss.

CHAPTER TEN

Motor: Scale, Price and Claims Discipline

Motor is the line many professionals underestimate because it is familiar. Familiarity should make us more careful, not less. Motor combines compulsory insurance, mass pricing, claims frequency, repair economics, fraud controls, consumer expectations and increasingly sophisticated data. Small errors are multiplied by volume.

In both the UAE and Saudi Arabia, motor regulation has moved toward standardised policy forms and stronger supervisory intervention. That makes operational discipline as important as technical knowledge. The broker who treats motor as an administrative product eventually discovers that administration is where much of the risk lives.

10.1 Compulsory insurance and market scale

Motor is one of the Gulf's highest-volume insurance classes and the line through which many customers experience insurance most directly. Compulsory third-party liability creates a regulatory floor; comprehensive cover, fleet structures and service arrangements create the commercial market above it.

For a corporate broker, fleets are where motor becomes technically interesting. Hundreds of repeated exposures generate enough claims history to reveal patterns in driver behaviour, vehicle use, repair cost, route design and deductible structure. That makes fleet broking a useful bridge between insurance procurement and practical risk management.

10.2 Liability, claims and standard forms

Compulsory motor insurance is a statutory product before it is a commercial one. The UAE and Saudi Arabia each operate regulator-prescribed compulsory motor frameworks, but the forms, limits, claims procedures and available extensions are not interchangeable. A broker working across the region must verify the current local wording rather than import assumptions from a neighbouring market.

Standardisation also does not make every insurer equivalent. Claims accessibility, repair arrangements, fraud controls, service response and the handling of exceptions continue to shape the insured experience. For corporate fleets, the compulsory policy is therefore only the floor. The broader programme still has to address vehicle values, use, driver profile, deductibles, repair strategy and loss control.

The Kuwait Construction Fleet: Fleet Excess Structure and Claims Frequency. A major Kuwaiti construction company operated a fleet of over three hundred vehicles including heavy trucks, cranes, and site vehicles. The company had historically purchased comprehensive motor fleet insurance with a nil deductible, resulting in a high volume of small claims and consistently elevated premiums at renewal. The broker recommended restructuring the programme with a KWD 500 self-insured retention on own-damage claims, combined with improved driver training and incident reporting procedures. The restructured programme reduced the total cost of risk, insurance premium plus retained claims cost, by a material amount in the first year, while improving the claims profile presented to the market at the following renewal. The broking lesson: The optimal motor fleet programme is not necessarily the one with the lowest premium. For large corporate fleets, introducing a self-insured retention on own-damage claims combined with risk management improvements can reduce the total cost of risk while improving the claims profile available for renewal negotiation. This is genuine risk management advice, not simply coverage placement.

10.3 What regulation changes in practice

The UAE continues to operate unified motor policy frameworks for third-party liability and loss and damage, while Saudi Arabia maintains a unified compulsory motor policy and separate comprehensive motor rules. Standardisation protects consumers and makes the product easier to compare, but it does not eliminate the broker's responsibility. Repair networks, claims service, deductibles, optional benefits, vehicle use, driver profile and insurer handling quality still matter.

10.4 The motor product is becoming a data product

Motor underwriting has always relied on data, but the granularity is increasing. Vehicle databases, claims histories, repair costs, telematics and fraud analytics can all influence price and claims handling. That makes data quality a broking issue. A wrong vehicle specification, use classification or driver profile can affect both premium and claim outcome.

Claims service remains the strongest differentiator for many customers. Repair-network quality, parts availability, surveyor turnaround and communication can matter more than a small premium saving. In fleet business, frequency analysis is particularly useful. A fleet with repeated low-severity losses may benefit more from driver management and deductible redesign than from another marketing exercise.

The broker who can show the client where losses occur, which vehicle groups drive frequency and what interventions might change the pattern is no longer selling motor insurance. They are helping manage fleet risk.

10.5 Fleet business is a risk-management laboratory

A corporate fleet gives the broker something individual motor rarely provides: enough repeated experience to distinguish pattern from accident. Frequency by vehicle type, location, driver group, time of day and cause can reveal a risk-management problem long before it becomes a pricing crisis.

I have worked on fleet presentations where the instinct was to compare quotations first. The more useful conversation began with the claims. If loss ratios are deteriorating, another market may provide temporary relief, but the underlying behaviour follows the fleet. Driver training, route management, telematics, repair controls, excess structure and claims triage can become part of the renewal strategy.

A high deductible can reduce premium but create administrative noise if the fleet has many small accidents. A low deductible can transfer routine cost while leaving the insurer to price the frequency. Neither is universally right. The structure should reflect the client's ability to retain predictable loss and the insurer's appetite for severity.

10.6 From practice: a Saudi fleet comparison

In 2026 my team prepared a multi-insurer motor fleet comparison for a corporate client in Saudi Arabia through a local broking relationship. The exercise reinforced a point I have made throughout this book: a comparison is useful only if it makes unlike quotations genuinely comparable.

We did not treat the number at the bottom of each offer as the conclusion. The presentation had to distinguish insurer terms, scope, deductibles, servicing assumptions and the practical differences behind the quotations. In a compulsory line, standard policy architecture can create the impression that every offer is interchangeable. Fleet reality proves otherwise. Claims service, repair arrangements, driver and vehicle schedules, and the discipline of the data supplied to the market can change the client's experience materially.

That is the difference between quote collection and broking. One produces alternatives. The other makes the alternatives intelligible.

CHAPTER ELEVEN

Health, Life and Employee Benefits

Health insurance is where regulation, medicine, employment, customer experience and data meet. It is also one of the lines in which a broker can most easily become an administrator instead of an adviser. The renewal file arrives with census data, utilisation reports and a premium increase. The temptation is to negotiate the increase and move on. The professional opportunity is much larger.

11.1 The Gulf moved from optional benefit to social infrastructure

Mandatory health insurance has been one of the most important structural changes in Gulf insurance. Dubai and Abu Dhabi developed mandatory systems earlier, but from 1 January 2025 the UAE extended mandatory health insurance to private-sector employees and domestic workers in Sharjah, Ajman, Umm Al Quwain, Ras Al Khaimah and Fujairah as residency permits are issued or renewed. That completed a national direction toward health coverage for the private-sector workforce, although the regulatory architecture and benefit structures still differ by emirate.

Dubai's scale shows what this means operationally. The Dubai Health Authority reported that beneficiaries under the emirate's health insurance system exceeded 4.9 million in 2025, while claims reached roughly 49.6 million. At that volume, network design, fraud controls, digital approvals, pharmacy management and provider behaviour are not side issues. They are the product experience.

Saudi Arabia's health insurance responsibilities transferred to the Insurance Authority in March 2024. For employers and brokers, the significance is not only that the name of the supervisor changed. Health is now part of a unified insurance regulatory agenda that also covers actuarial pricing, market conduct, digitalisation and insurer stability.

11.2 A medical policy is a network before it is a schedule

Clients naturally compare limits, co-payments and exclusions. Employees experience the policy through something more concrete: can I reach a good doctor when I need one? A technically generous schedule attached to a poor or inconvenient provider network can be a weak benefit. A slightly narrower schedule with strong network access, reliable approvals and sensible chronic-condition management can create better real-world value.

That is why I ask HR teams to look beyond the premium and the top-line benefit table. Where do employees actually live and work? Which hospitals and clinics do they use? What proportion of claims is outpatient, pharmacy, dental, optical or inpatient? Are dependants driving a different utilisation pattern from employees? Where are high-cost cases concentrated? Which diagnoses are recurring? What does the denial data say?

11.3 From my own claims analytics

In 2026 we reviewed a UAE group medical programme for a trading and commodities business. Membership had grown from 253 to 285 lives. The raw claims number was already large, but the useful insight came from disaggregation. Processed claims were about AED 1.69 million and estimated exposure, after allowing for pending claims and IBNR, was just over AED 2 million. Outpatient spend dominated. Pharmacy represented more than one-fifth of claims value, and spouses and dependants together accounted for almost half of total spend.

The answer was not simply to ask the insurer for a lower renewal rate. The data pointed toward practical interventions: better pharmacy controls, musculoskeletal management, review of referral pathways, closer monitoring of high-frequency outpatient use and more deliberate member communication. That is the difference between broking a premium and broking a risk.

11.4 The renewal conversation that matters

Medical renewals often become emotionally difficult because the buyer sees a budget and the insurer sees a loss ratio. Both are real. The broker's job is to convert the argument into evidence.

A credible renewal conversation should separate utilisation from medical inflation, membership changes, large one-off claims, chronic cases, network leakage, benefit design and insurer margin. If the loss ratio deteriorated because membership grew or because one exceptional oncology claim occurred, that tells a different story from a programme with persistent high-frequency utilisation and weak controls. Underwriters price stories differently when the data supports the distinction.

11.5 Life and protection benefits

Group life remains simpler operationally than medical, but the simplicity can be deceptive. Salary multiples, free-cover limits, medical underwriting, actively-at-work provisions, territorial scope and beneficiary administration all deserve careful review. Where workmen's compensation, employers' liability and group life overlap, the broker should explain the different purposes rather than assume the client understands them.

The principle is the same across benefits: the schedule is not the benefit. The benefit is what happens to an employee or family when they need it.

11.6 Medical renewal is increasingly an analytics conversation

Medical insurance produces a volume of data that can either illuminate the programme or overwhelm the client. The broker's job is to find the few patterns that change a decision. Utilisation by benefit, high-cost claimants, chronic conditions, provider concentration, pharmacy spend, out-of-network use, member growth and claims development can each matter, but not every chart deserves equal attention.

I prefer to begin with the question the client will face at renewal: what is driving the insurer's view of our future cost? That forces analysis away from decoration. A rising loss ratio can come from a genuine deterioration in morbidity, a one-off large claimant, membership growth, benefit richness, inflation, provider behaviour or incomplete IBNR. Those causes deserve different responses.

The regional medical market also reminds us that insurance is a service network. A theoretically attractive benefit schedule can fail if employees cannot access the right hospitals or clinics where they live and work. In Saudi Arabia, a workforce spread across Riyadh, Jeddah and the Eastern Province can have very different practical needs. In the UAE, the same issue appears between emirates and among provider networks. The broker should test network adequacy against workforce geography, not against the length of the provider list.

11.7 Prevention is becoming part of broking

Wellness is easy to market and difficult to evaluate. A health screening campaign, chronic-disease programme or telemedicine benefit should not be treated as valuable simply because it sounds progressive. The serious question is whether it changes access, behaviour, cost or health outcomes for the population being insured.

For employers, the most useful interventions are often targeted rather than broad. If claims analytics show musculoskeletal conditions driving outpatient cost, a focused physiotherapy or ergonomics programme may be more relevant than a generic wellness calendar. If pharmacy dominates, formulary and chronic-condition management deserve attention. If dependants account for a large share of utilisation, communication and preventive screening should include families rather than focusing only on employees.

This is where the broker's role can move beyond annual procurement. The policy remains necessary, but the more interesting work is helping the client understand what the claims are saying about the workforce and what can be changed before the next renewal.

CHAPTER TWELVE

Energy, Construction and Infrastructure

Few insurance programmes reveal the difference between product knowledge and risk knowledge as clearly as energy, construction and infrastructure. A broker can know every standard clause and still be unprepared for the engineering reality of a project.

In these risks, the quality of the submission depends on understanding what is being built or operated, the contractual allocation of responsibility, the critical path, testing and commissioning, surrounding property, natural hazards, contractor interfaces and the financial consequences of delay. Technical specialists matter, but the broker's role remains to connect those specialist views into one coherent risk story.

12.1 Energy: where engineering and insurance meet

Insurance for the energy sector in the GCC represents one of the most technically demanding and commercially significant areas of the regional market. The oil, gas, and petrochemical industries generate insurance requirements on a scale and with a technical complexity that makes energy insurance a true specialist discipline. Upstream energy insurance covers exploration and production activities; downstream covers refining, processing, storage, and distribution. Both require specialist technical knowledge of operations, risk management standards, and engineering benchmarks.

12.2 Construction risk across the project life cycle

The GCC has been the site of some of the world's most ambitious construction programmes, and the pace of development shows no sign of moderating under Vision 2030 in Saudi Arabia, the UAE's diversification agenda, and equivalent national programmes across the Gulf. The construction insurance broker must advise clients at every stage of the project lifecycle, from pre-construction risk assessment through the construction period, testing and commissioning, and the transition to operational coverage.

Regional Case Study

The Saudi Petrochemical Project: Delay in Start-Up Coverage

A major new petrochemical complex in the Kingdom completed physical construction and moved into the testing and commissioning phase. The contractors all risks policy provided coverage during the construction period but was structured to terminate at practical completion. The operational property programme was not due to incept until the facility achieved the agreed commissioning milestone. During commissioning, a significant equipment failure in the heat exchanger train delayed first production by four months. During this period, neither the CAR policy (which had terminated at practical completion) nor the operational property policy (which had not yet incepted) responded to the business interruption loss arising from the delay. Why it matters: The gap between the end of contractors all risks coverage and the inception of operational coverage is a well-known but frequently mismanaged exposure. Delay in Start-Up (DSU) insurance specifically addresses the business interruption losses arising from commissioning delays. For major industrial projects, DSU should be considered as a standard element of the project insurance programme, not as an optional addition.

12.3 Delay in start-up deserves its own conversation

Construction clients naturally focus on physical damage because the project is visible. The financial consequence of delay can be larger. Delay in start-up or advance loss of profits cover is designed around that consequence, but it is one of the easiest covers to misunderstand.

The insured value depends on forecast financial performance. The indemnity period depends on the time required to recover the project schedule after an insured event. Critical-path analysis matters because damage to a non-critical component may not delay completion while damage to one specialised item can move the whole project. Suppliers can be as important as the site itself.

A serious DSU discussion therefore involves the project team, finance, contractors and the broker. It is not a percentage added to the CAR premium. The broker should understand which milestones drive revenue, which equipment has long lead times, what contingency exists in the schedule and how an insured delay would actually reach the client's income statement.

12.4 The submission should read like an engineering story

Complex engineering submissions fail when they are long but not informative. Hundreds of pages of drawings and contracts do not automatically answer the underwriter's questions. The broker and technical team have to extract the risk story: what is being built, who is responsible, what has been built before, which phases are critical, what natural hazards exist, how testing will occur, where values accumulate and what could create a large delay.

For energy risks the same principle applies to operations. Maintenance philosophy, redundancy, loss history, inspection, process safety and emergency response are not ancillary information. They are part of the risk quality the insurer is pricing.

A good technical submission therefore has two levels. The executive layer lets an underwriter understand the risk quickly. The technical appendices let specialists verify the detail. Confusing those levels either produces a superficial submission or buries the important information inside a data room.

12.5 Project insurance is a governance mechanism

Large projects contain many parties with different incentives: owner, main contractor, subcontractors, lenders, consultants, suppliers and operators. Insurance can reduce the friction among them by creating a common programme, but only if the insured parties, waivers, deductibles and responsibility for uninsured loss are aligned with the contracts.

The broker should therefore sit close to the contractual architecture. When a project contract changes, insurance may need to change with it. When a new contractor is introduced, when ownership is novated, or when a section is handed over early, the programme should be tested rather than assumed to have followed automatically.

CHAPTER THIRTEEN

Political Risk, Credit, Cyber and Emerging Cover

Some risks refuse to sit neatly inside traditional categories. Political intervention can stop a payment without damaging an asset. A customer can fail financially without any physical event. A cyber incident can begin as an IT problem and end as business interruption, liability, extortion and reputational harm. These are the lines that teach a broker to think beyond the policy label.

They are also the lines most sensitive to changes in geopolitics, technology and contract structure. The professional habit is therefore not to memorise a product description, but to understand the mechanism of loss.

13.1 Political risk: when the state becomes part of the loss

Political risk insurance covers losses arising from political events that disrupt commercial activities or damage commercial assets. For businesses with operations or investments in the broader Middle East, beyond the more stable GCC core, political risk insurance is a practical necessity, not a theoretical product. Coverage categories include expropriation and nationalisation, political violence including war and civil unrest, currency inconvertibility and transfer restriction, contract frustration by a government counterparty, and import or export embargo.

The Egyptian Investment and Currency Inconvertibility. A GCC-based conglomerate held a significant manufacturing investment in Egypt. Following a period of currency pressure, the Egyptian regulatory authorities imposed restrictions on the repatriation of foreign currency profits by foreign-owned entities. The restriction was not an expropriation, the investment itself was unaffected, but it effectively prevented the GCC investor from accessing the dividend income from its Egyptian operations for an extended period. The investor held political risk insurance that included a currency inconvertibility and transfer restriction coverage extension. The insurer confirmed coverage and the investor was able to claim compensation for the delayed repatriation during the period of restriction. Without the political risk policy, the financial impact would have been absorbed entirely by the investor. What mattered: Currency inconvertibility and transfer restriction is one of the most frequently triggered political risk coverage categories in the MENA region, yet it is one of the least understood by corporate clients who have not previously suffered its effects. The broker advising GCC corporates with investments or operations across the broader Middle East should include political risk assessment in every commercial insurance review.

13.2 Trade credit: insuring the balance sheet

Trade credit insurance covers the risk that a business's debtors will fail to pay amounts owed for goods delivered or services rendered, due to insolvency or protracted default. For businesses operating in the GCC, where extended payment terms are common and where economic conditions can affect debtor creditworthiness significantly, trade credit insurance represents a meaningful commercial risk management tool. The GCC trade credit insurance market has grown as regional businesses have integrated more deeply into international supply chains and adopted more sophisticated credit management practices.

13.3 Cyber: a policy built around response

Cyber insurance is one of the fastest-growing lines of commercial insurance in the GCC, reflecting the region's rapid digital transformation, the increasing frequency and sophistication of cyberattacks, and the growing recognition among corporate boards that cyber risk represents one of the most significant operational threats facing businesses today. Book Four of this series, Risk Ecosystem Entanglement, addresses the systemic dimensions of cyber risk in the GCC and global context in significant detail.

Regional Case Study

The UAE Financial Services Firm: Cyber Incident and the Insurance Response

A UAE-licensed financial services firm suffered a ransomware attack that encrypted its client data systems and demanded a cryptocurrency ransom. The firm held a cyber insurance policy that covered ransomware response costs including forensic investigation, system restoration, ransom negotiation, and business interruption. The insurer's incident response service was activated within hours, providing the firm with access to specialist cybersecurity forensic experts and a ransomware negotiation service. The incident was contained within seventy-two hours, a ransom payment was agreed at a significantly lower amount than initially demanded, and systems were restored. The total insured cost, forensics, ransom payment, and business interruption, was substantially below what the firm would have borne without coverage. The broking lesson: The value of cyber insurance is most visible when an incident actually occurs and the insurer's response services are activated. The broker advising on cyber insurance should focus the client's attention not only on the financial coverage but on the quality and speed of the incident response services the insurer provides, because in a real cyber incident, the response capability often matters more than the policy limit.

13.4 Cyber is increasingly an operational service contract

The most useful cyber policies are not merely indemnity instruments. They create access to incident response, forensic expertise, legal advice, notification support, negotiation capability and business interruption assessment. That changes how the broker should compare products. Two policies with similar headline limits can produce very different outcomes at 2 a.m. during a ransomware event.

13.5 Emerging risk is often old risk in a new chain

The phrase 'emerging risk' can make ordinary professionals feel they need a new vocabulary for everything. Often the better approach is to trace the loss chain. A cloud outage is new technology, but its financial consequence may still be business interruption. A deepfake-enabled fraud is technologically novel, but the loss may sit somewhere between crime, cyber and professional liability. Climate change may alter frequency and severity, while the policy questions remain property damage, interruption, liability and availability of capacity.

This does not mean existing products are always sufficient. It means product innovation should begin with the mechanism of loss rather than fashion. Ask what event occurs, who suffers loss, which balance sheet is affected, whether physical damage is required, whether liability is alleged, what exclusions apply and which policy is intended to respond. The chain reveals where the traditional programme breaks.

The broker's advantage is not predicting every new risk. It is being able to reason through unfamiliar risk without waiting for a market brochure to explain it.

13.6 Cyber insurance is purchased in peace and used in crisis

The most important part of a cyber policy may be the telephone number the client calls at two in the morning. Modern cyber insurance often bundles access to forensic investigators, breach counsel, negotiators, public-relations support, notification services and recovery specialists. That makes vendor panels and incident-response procedures part of the insurance product.

The broker should test whether the client's own incident-response plan understands the policy. Who is authorised to contact the insurer? Can the client appoint its preferred forensic firm, or must it use the panel? What happens if an emergency vendor is engaged before consent? Which territories and privacy regimes are relevant? How does the business interruption waiting period operate? These questions are much easier before encryption appears on the screen.

Cyber also exposes programme overlap. A ransomware event can involve crime, property, professional liability, D&O and cyber cover. A social-engineering loss can sit awkwardly between cyber and crime. A technology outage can cause contingent business interruption without malicious activity. The broker should map the event across the programme rather than assume the policy with 'cyber' in its title owns every digital loss.

13.7 Political and credit risk are really about cash-flow interruption

Political risk and trade credit can look exotic because the triggers are legal or political rather than physical. For the client, the consequence is often more ordinary: cash that was expected does not arrive. A government restricts transfer. A buyer becomes insolvent. A contract is frustrated. A licence is revoked. The balance sheet absorbs the interruption.

This perspective helps brokers explain specialist products to finance teams. The discussion becomes less about unusual insurance language and more about receivables, investment value, debt service and liquidity. Specialist cover becomes relevant when the financial exposure is understood first.

PART THREE

DOING THE WORK

Placement, relationships, negotiation and claims are where technical knowledge becomes professional value.

CHAPTER FOURTEEN

Risk Placement: Turning Exposure into a Market Story

Placement is often described as the moment a broker goes to market. I think it begins much earlier. It begins when the broker decides what the risk actually is, what evidence will make an underwriter comfortable, and which aspects of the client's story require challenge rather than presentation.

I have seen mediocre risks receive strong terms because the submission was honest, organised and technically persuasive. I have also seen attractive risks underperform because the submission looked like a data dump. Underwriters are not buying a presentation; they are accepting uncertainty. Good broking reduces the uncertainty that does not need to be there.

14.1 Placement starts before the market sees the risk

The placement of an insurance risk is a structured professional process that encompasses multiple distinct stages. Risk understanding: the systematic gathering and analysis of information about the client's operations, assets, activities, and exposures. Risk assessment: the professional analysis of the risk profile to identify material exposures, their probable severity and frequency, and the coverage requirements they generate. Market strategy: the selection of appropriate insurers, the preparation of a compelling and complete risk presentation, and the development of a negotiation strategy. Placement: the agreement of terms, confirmation of coverage, and preparation of documentation that accurately reflects the agreed terms.

14.2 The questions before the quotation

A thorough risk assessment is the foundation of every professional placement. It should cover the nature of the business, the physical characteristics of insured property, the operational exposures, the loss history, and the risk management arrangements in place. The risk assessment should not be passive, it should be an active professional enquiry in which the broker uses their knowledge and experience to probe systematically for information relevant to the coverage design and the market presentation.

Regional Case Study

The Doha Hotel: The Risk Assessment Gap

A broker renewed a property and liability programme for a major Doha hotel without conducting an updated risk survey. In the preceding year, the hotel had added a rooftop bar and swimming pool, significantly increasing its public liability exposure profile, and had commenced significant renovation works in one wing, creating a contractors liability exposure during the renovation period. Neither the rooftop extension nor the renovation works were reflected in the renewal submission. When a guest was injured in an incident linked to the renovation area, the insurer queried whether the risk as renewed accurately reflected the operations as they existed at the time of the incident. The broking lesson: The risk assessment obligation is not a one-time exercise at programme inception: it must be repeated at every renewal and triggered by any material change in the client's operations. The broker who treats renewal as an administrative process without reassessing the risk profile is not meeting their professional obligations.

14.3 The submission is an underwriting tool

The market submission is the document through which the broker presents the client's risk to insurers. A professional submission is accurate, complete, well-organised, and compelling. It is accurate in the sense that all information presented is true and consistent with available documentation. It is complete in the sense that all material facts relevant to the underwriter's assessment have been included. It is well-organised in a logical structure that allows efficient underwriting assessment. And it is compelling in that it presents the risk's positive characteristics in a way that distinguishes it from others the underwriter is reviewing.

14.4 Market strategy, not market shopping

Negotiation with underwriters in the GCC reflects the relationship-centric commercial culture of the region. The underwriter who knows the broker, trusts the broker's professional judgement, and respects the broker's standing in the market is more likely to provide capacity for a challenging risk and to apply flexibility in difficult situations. Relationship capital is a real and valuable professional asset, built through years of honest professional conduct and not manufactured through social entertainment.

From My Experience

The submission is part of the negotiation

I once watched a technically strong risk struggle in the market because the presentation made the underwriter work too hard to understand it. The broker had provided the information, but not the story. The next version of the submission did not hide anything and did not add marketing language. It reorganised the facts around the underwriter's real concerns: fire protection, business interruption dependency, claims history, risk improvements and management response. The quality of the market conversation changed immediately. That experience stayed with me. Completeness is not the same as clarity. A market submission should reduce the underwriter's uncertainty, not simply transfer the client's document archive into another inbox.

14.5 The market strategy belongs on one page

Before a major placement goes to market, I like the team to be able to explain the strategy on one page. What are we asking insurers to cover? Which terms are non-negotiable for the client? Which markets genuinely fit the risk? What is the incumbent's position? Where do we expect resistance? What evidence can reduce that resistance? What alternatives exist if the first strategy fails?

This discipline prevents a placement from becoming a sequence of unrelated emails. It also helps the team know when new information changes the strategy. If one market introduces a wording improvement the client values more than price, the broker can decide whether to use that development with other markets. If capacity tightens, the team can decide whether to restructure layers rather than continue asking the same question.

A renewal meeting with the client should then explain the strategy, not simply present the outcome. Clients become better insurance buyers when they understand why the market responded as it did. Better buyers make better long-term clients.

14.6 The submission should disclose the problem, not hide it

One of the fastest ways to lose underwriting confidence is to make the underwriter discover the bad news. A major loss, combustible construction, weak controls or an adverse contract does not become less real because it appears on page eighty rather than page two. In difficult risks, credibility often improves when the broker states the weakness clearly and then explains what has been done about it.

This matters because underwriting is not a search for perfect risks. Perfect risks are rare and, if they existed, they would not need much insurance. Underwriters are deciding whether uncertainty is understood and priced. A broker who identifies the weakness, quantifies it where possible and presents mitigation gives the market something it can work with.

I have seen submissions improved dramatically by one honest paragraph: here is the loss, here is why it happened, here is what changed afterward, and here is the evidence. That paragraph can be more persuasive than twenty pages of generic company profile.

14.7 Market selection is part of negotiation

Sending every risk to every insurer is not automatically thorough. It can be a sign that no strategy exists. A market that has no appetite for the exposure will waste time. A market that receives poorly targeted submissions repeatedly may also become less responsive when a suitable risk finally arrives.

The broker should know which insurers can lead, which can follow, which have the relevant technical expertise, which need facultative support and which are useful as competitive alternatives. The strategy can change once indications arrive, but it should begin with a view.

There is also a client-management benefit. When the client understands why particular markets were approached and why others were not, the process becomes more transparent. The broker is no longer a black box between client and insurer. That transparency is increasingly important as regulation and procurement both ask advisers to demonstrate how recommendations were reached.

14.8 A quotation is not an answer

Common Professional Mistakes

1. Treating renewal as administration instead of reassessing the risk.
2. Sending the risk to every market without a deliberate strategy.
3. Presenting positive features while burying adverse information.
4. Comparing premium before scope, exclusions, limits and insurer quality.
5. Failing to document why the final recommendation was made.

I tell teams to compare quotations in the order a claim might reveal their differences: scope, exclusions, limits and sublimits, deductibles, conditions, insurer quality and claims service, then price. Commercial reality sometimes forces a different priority, but the discipline prevents premium from becoming the only visible variable.

The final recommendation should also say what remains imperfect. There are renewals where no market will provide the ideal wording. There are clients whose budget will not support the preferred limit. There are risks where the technically strongest insurer is materially more expensive. Professional advice does not require pretending those trade-offs do not exist. It requires making them explicit enough that the client can decide.

> *A good submission gives an underwriter reasons to say yes. A great submission also tells the underwriter where the difficulties are, before the underwriter has to discover them.*

CHAPTER FIFTEEN

Trust, Culture and the Client Relationship

People sometimes describe the GCC as a 'relationship market' as though that means personal connection can substitute for technical work. It cannot. Relationship helps most when the technical work is already credible.

Trust in this market is cumulative. An underwriter remembers whether the last submission was accurate. A client remembers whether you returned the difficult call, not only the renewal meeting. A regulator remembers whether the evidence arrived when promised. Hospitality, courtesy and cultural intelligence matter, but the relationship that survives pressure is built from competence repeated over time.

15.1 Culture matters, but not in the way stereotypes suggest

The commercial culture of the GCC and Middle East is built upon foundations distinctively different from those of Western commercial environments. Cultural competence in this market is not a soft skill that supplements technical knowledge. It is a professional skill as essential as knowledge of the lines of business.

The concept of wasta, which broadly translates as influence, connection, or the use of personal relationships to facilitate commercial and social outcomes, is fundamental to understanding how business gets done in the GCC. In a market where decisions are made by individuals who have relationships with other individuals, and where those relationships carry moral weight, the broker who is well-connected and respected can access opportunities and achieve outcomes simply unavailable to those without equivalent relational capital. Wasta amplifies competence; it cannot substitute for it.

Trust, expressed in Arabic as thiqa, is perhaps even more fundamental. The broker who consistently demonstrates trustworthiness through honest communication, reliable delivery on commitments, transparent handling of remuneration and conflicts of interest, and genuine prioritisation of the client's interests will build a professional reputation that generates sustainable commercial success. Trust takes years to build and can be destroyed in a single interaction.

15.2 Communication, hierarchy and difficult conversations

Professional communication in the GCC business environment tends to be more indirect and relationship-contextual than the direct, transactional communication style of much Western business practice. Disagreement may be expressed through silence, through a change of subject, or through a form of qualified agreement that carries an implicit reservation rather than through direct refusal. The management of face, the preservation of the dignity and social standing of all parties, is a constant consideration.

For the insurance broker, this means that advice about coverage gaps, inadequate sums insured, or inadequate risk management must be delivered in ways that allow the client to hear and act upon the advice without feeling publicly criticised or undermined. Initial meetings typically have a significant relationship-building component before substantive business discussion begins. Investing time in genuine conversation before moving to the business agenda is not wasted time, it is the professional work of building the relationship within which business advice will be heard and acted upon.

The Kuwaiti Family Business: Advice Delivered Well. A broker needed to advise a senior member of a Kuwaiti family business that the company's property insurance programme was significantly underinsured and that the public liability limits were inadequate for the scale of the company's current operations, which had grown substantially since the programme was last reviewed. Rather than presenting this as a list of programme deficiencies in a formal written report, the broker requested a private meeting with the appropriate senior family member, not a committee meeting, and framed the conversation around the company's success and growth rather than around failures in the insurance programme. The advice was delivered as a recognition of how much the business had grown and a professional recommendation to ensure the insurance programme reflected that growth. The client received and acted upon the advice fully. The practical point: The substance of professional advice does not change with cultural context. The delivery does. In the GCC, advice that would be routinely delivered in a direct, transactional style in some other markets must often be framed with greater care for relationship context, timing, and the preservation of dignity. The broker who masters this skill delivers the same quality of advice more effectively.

15.3 Respect is more useful than stereotypes

Cultural intelligence is real, but it is damaged by simplistic rules about how 'Gulf clients' or 'Arab businesspeople' behave. The region contains family enterprises, listed companies, government entities, multinationals, technology firms and professional partnerships. Age, nationality, ownership and corporate culture can matter as much as geography.

The useful principles are more modest. Learn who actually decides. Respect hierarchy without using it as an excuse to avoid difficult advice. Understand that trust may be established through repeated personal contact rather than purely formal procurement. Do not embarrass a client publicly when a private conversation would solve the problem. Keep commitments. Follow up. And never mistake warmth for agreement.

A strong relationship gives a broker permission to tell the client something unwelcome. That is one of its highest values. If a relationship can survive only positive news, it is not yet trust.

15.4 The difficult conversation is part of the relationship

A broker earns little professional credit for agreeing with everything the client wants. Some of the most important meetings involve telling a respected client that the limit is inadequate, the disclosure is incomplete, the insurer is unsuitable, or the requested saving cannot be achieved without weakening cover.

How that advice is delivered matters. In relationship-led markets, bluntness can be mistaken for strength and excessive diplomacy can hide the message. I prefer clarity with respect. State the issue, explain the consequence, offer alternatives and leave the client with a decision rather than an accusation.

There is also a moment when the broker has to accept that advice can be rejected. The file should record the recommendation and the client's decision without turning the relationship into a legal notice. A mature professional can disagree with the client and still serve the client well.

15.5 Service is remembered in the gaps between renewals

The easiest way for a brokerage to become transactional is to organise the entire client relationship around expiry dates. The client then hears from the broker when information is needed, when premium is due and when the renewal presentation is ready. Everything feels efficient and strangely one-sided.

The strongest relationships have another rhythm. Claims reviews, stewardship meetings, regulatory updates, risk surveys, claims analytics and mid-term coverage changes create contact around the client's business rather than the broker's renewal calendar. This is not activity for its own sake. Each interaction should answer a real question or improve the programme.

Over time those conversations give the broker context that no proposal form can capture. When renewal arrives, less of the client's story has to be rediscovered.

CHAPTER SIXTEEN

Negotiating with Underwriters

Negotiation is not the art of asking for a lower number until somebody agrees. The strongest negotiations change the underwriter's view of the risk or change the structure of the deal.

Sometimes the correct move is to improve a deductible, narrow an exclusion, obtain a longer reporting period, increase a sublimit or change the basis of valuation rather than chase another small premium reduction. A broker who negotiates only price is negotiating the easiest part of the contract.

16.1 See the risk from the other side of the table

Effective negotiation with underwriters begins not with the broker's objectives but with a genuine understanding of the underwriter's perspective. The underwriter is assessing the quality of the risk itself, the quality of the broker's submission, and the commercial context of the relationship. The broker who structures their approach to help the underwriter satisfy all three dimensions simultaneously is in a far stronger negotiating position than the broker who focuses only on premium and coverage terms.

16.2 Relationships that survive a difficult risk

In the GCC insurance market, the relationship between the broker and the underwriter is a professional relationship with significant commercial value. Underwriters allocate their capacity, their analytical attention, and their flexibility on the basis of their confidence in the brokers they work with. This confidence is earned through consistent professional conduct: presenting risks accurately (including their negative characteristics), not approaching markets with risks that are not appropriate for them, following through on commitments, and being honest when circumstances change.

The Abu Dhabi Industrial Risk: The Value of a Trusted Relationship. A broker was asked to place a challenging industrial risk with a significant loss history that had made several local insurers reluctant to renew on acceptable terms. The risk was technically sound, with strong risk management improvements since the prior losses, but the loss history made it a difficult placement in a market that was generally cautious. The broker approached a senior underwriter at a local insurer with whom they had a long-standing professional relationship based on consistent and accurate risk presentations over many years. The underwriter agreed to review the risk in detail based on the broker's professional recommendation rather than declining on the basis of the loss history alone. Following a technical site visit, the insurer agreed to renew on commercially acceptable terms. Why it matters: Professional relationship capital with underwriters generates tangible commercial outcomes in difficult market situations. The broker who has invested consistently in honest and accurate market relationships can achieve results for challenging clients that are simply not available to brokers who have not made that investment. This is one of the most concrete commercial returns on professional conduct.

16.3 Negotiating beyond premium

A renewal negotiation has more than one currency. Premium matters, but so do deductible, limit, sublimit, waiting period, wording breadth, claims protocol, security requirements, reinstatement provisions, territorial scope and the duration of rate commitments. When the market will not move on price, the broker should know which other term creates the most value for this client.

16.4 The psychology of a credible ask

Underwriters receive many requests framed as urgency: 'the client needs it today', 'the competitor has done better', 'please support us'. Urgency is real, but it is not underwriting evidence. A credible request connects the concession being sought to a reason.

If you want a lower deductible, explain the risk controls and claims experience. If you want an exclusion deleted, explain why the exposure is limited or how it is managed. If you want a lower rate, show the portfolio performance, improvements or competitive context. If you need a rapid turnaround, provide a clean submission that respects the underwriter's time.

The quality of the ask influences the quality of the response. Over time, underwriters learn which brokers ask for everything and which brokers know what matters. That reputation becomes negotiating capital.

16.5 Negotiation has a memory

Underwriters remember how a broker behaved on previous placements. Did the broker disclose the adverse fact early? Did they bind when they said they would? Did they use an indication merely to shop the market? Did they bring sensible business, or only impossible requests with no supporting information? Those memories influence the next conversation even when nobody writes them into a score.

That is why negotiation should protect future credibility. Threatening to move an account can work once. Repeatedly using the threat without moving it weakens the next request. Claiming a competitor has offered a term that does not exist may win a concession and lose a relationship. Short-term tactics have a long memory in a relatively concentrated regional market.

The strongest negotiating leverage is optionality built honestly: credible alternative markets, a well-prepared risk, a client willing to improve controls, and enough time before expiry to use those options.

16.6 Know when to stop negotiating

There is a point at which another round creates more risk than value. Terms can expire, underwriter patience can thin, and a strong offer can be destabilised while the broker searches for a marginal improvement. Good negotiation includes knowing when the client's objectives have been met sufficiently to bind.

That judgement should be discussed with the client. The broker negotiates; the client owns the commercial decision. When time is short, the distinction becomes especially important.

CHAPTER SEVENTEEN

Claims Advocacy: Where Broking Is Tested

Claims are where every earlier decision becomes visible. A weak disclosure, an ambiguous endorsement, an unrealistic value, a missing extension or a poor insurer choice can remain invisible for months. Then a loss occurs and the file becomes a record of everything that was done well and everything that was not.

I have always believed that claims advocacy is the broker's finest hour, but that phrase can be misunderstood. Advocacy is not aggression. It is not writing the longest letter or escalating every disagreement. The best advocacy is factual, timely and disciplined. It knows when to press, when to listen and when a quiet technical point is stronger than a dramatic argument.

17.1 The promise becomes a file

The insurance claim is the moment of truth for the insurance transaction. Every decision made during placement, the coverage terms negotiated, the exclusions accepted, the insurer selected, the risk information provided, becomes either a source of protection or a source of difficulty at the claims moment. The broker who has placed coverage professionally will find that the claims process confirms the value of that professional work. The broker who has placed coverage carelessly will find that the claims process exposes those failures in the most painful possible way.

In the GCC and Middle East, the claims environment has specific characteristics that make effective claims advocacy particularly important. The claims handling capabilities of local insurers vary significantly. The cultural norms around commercial dispute resolution mean that the formal legal route is not always the most effective or relationship-preserving mechanism for resolving a coverage dispute. And the broker's relationship with the insurer, built through years of professional interaction, can be a significant factor in the resolution of disputed claims.

17.2 The first 48 hours

When a client suffers a loss that may give rise to an insurance claim, the broker's first responsibility is immediate and practical: to help the client take the steps necessary to protect their position, preserve their rights under the policy, and initiate the claims process correctly. The broker must advise the client to notify the insurer promptly within the required timeframe, to take reasonable steps to minimise further loss, to preserve evidence of the loss and its cause, and to document the extent of the loss systematically.

17.3 The loss adjuster and the Broker's Advocacy Role

The loss adjuster appointed by the insurer to investigate and assess the claim is an independent professional acting on behalf of the insurer. The broker should facilitate the loss adjuster's access to information and to the client, while ensuring that the client understands that the loss adjuster represents the insurer's interests rather than the client's. The broker must review the loss adjuster's report carefully before it is accepted as the basis for settlement. Where the report contains factual errors, incorrect coverage analysis, or quantum assessments that do not reflect the actual loss, the broker should challenge them with appropriate documentation and professional argument.

Regional Case Study

The Manama Property Claim: Challenging the loss adjuster

A commercial property in Manama suffered fire damage to a section of the building. The loss adjuster appointed by the insurer assessed the claim and recommended a settlement based on depreciated value rather than reinstatement cost. The broker reviewed the loss adjuster's report and identified that the policy had been placed on a reinstatement basis, meaning the insurer's obligation was to pay the cost of reinstating the damaged structure on a like-for-like new basis, not the depreciated value. The broker prepared a written challenge to the loss adjuster's report, citing the specific reinstatement basis clause in the policy and providing a professional quantity surveyor's estimate of the actual reinstatement cost. The insurer accepted the challenge and the final settlement was significantly higher than the adjustor's initial recommendation. The practical point: The loss adjuster's report is not the final word on coverage or quantum. The broker's professional obligation is to review the report carefully and to challenge it whenever it contains errors of fact, incorrect coverage analysis, or quantum assessments inconsistent with the policy terms. This advocacy function is one of the most tangible demonstrations of the broker's professional value.

17.4 Challenge without losing the argument

Where the insurer declines a claim, or offers a settlement the client considers inadequate, the broker's role as claims advocate becomes critical. A professional claims dispute begins with a clear written statement of the coverage position: why the client believes the claim falls within the scope of coverage, referencing specific policy language and interpreting it in the manner most favourable to the client's position. It is supported by factual and technical evidence and explores the full range of available resolution mechanisms: internal escalation within the insurer, regulatory complaints processes, expert determination, and, as a last resort, litigation.

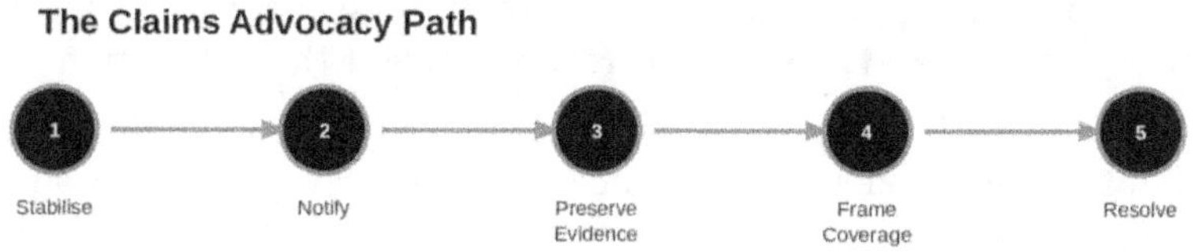

FIGURE 2 Claims advocacy is a sequence. Skipping the early disciplines makes later argument harder.

From My Experience

Sometimes the first advocacy move is restraint

A large UAE services company notified a professional indemnity matter. The temptation was to send a detailed coverage argument with the first notice because the client wanted reassurance immediately. We chose a lean notification instead: establish the facts, notify promptly, preserve rights and wait for the insurer's initial position before deploying every argument. That was not passivity. It was sequencing. Claims correspondence creates a record, and unnecessary argument can close doors before the insurer has even stated what it disputes. There are times to write the long letter. There are also times when the most professional move is to avoid answering a question nobody has yet asked.

17.5 When a claim becomes a coverage dispute

A disputed claim should be reduced to propositions that can be tested. What does the policy say? What facts are agreed? Which facts are disputed? What exclusion or condition is being relied upon? What evidence supports causation and quantum? Which jurisdiction's law matters? Once these questions are separated, emotion can be moved out of the centre of the file without ignoring the client's very real frustration.

17.6 Build the claim file as though someone else will inherit it

Large claims outlive people. Claims managers change, adjusters rotate, client finance teams move on and memories fade. The file has to survive the people who started it.

A good claim chronology is one of the simplest tools in complex claims. It records the event, notifications, meetings, document requests, submissions, insurer positions, payments, reservations and outstanding issues. It should distinguish fact from interpretation and show who is responsible for the next action.

Quantum deserves its own discipline. The broker should help the client understand what evidence the policy requires and should challenge unreasonable requests, but the claim is stronger when the financial presentation can be reconciled. In business interruption claims this may require accountants and forensic specialists. In major property losses it may require engineers, valuers and contractors. The broker's role is to keep the coverage, evidence and process aligned.

And one warning: a reservation of rights is not a claim denial. It may signal a serious coverage issue, but reacting as though the final decision has already been made can harden positions unnecessarily. Read what the insurer has actually said before arguing with what you fear it may say.

17.7 Claims advocacy starts at placement

The easiest claim to advocate is one whose coverage intention was made clear before the loss. If a critical extension was negotiated specifically for an exposure, keep the correspondence. If an underwriter accepted a risk feature after discussion, make sure the final wording reflects it. If the client disclosed a circumstance, retain evidence of the disclosure. The future claims file is partly created during placement.

This is one reason I dislike casual wording changes at the end of a renewal. A clause added at 6:45 p.m. to get the policy bound can become the centre of a multimillion-dirham dispute two years later. Urgency does not reduce the need to understand what was agreed.

17.8 The broker should manage the temperature of the room

Large claims create anxiety because money, operations and sometimes reputation are at stake. Clients can interpret questions as accusations. Insurers can become defensive when every information request is challenged. Experts can talk past each other. Someone has to keep the process technical enough to move.

The broker is well placed to do this because they understand the policy and the relationship, but only if they resist becoming theatrical. I have found that a clear chronology, a short list of disputed points and disciplined meeting notes often achieve more than an angry escalation. Escalation has a place. It is stronger when the file shows that the technical route was exhausted first.

17.9 Settlement is not the end of the claim

Common Professional Mistakes

1. Treating the adjuster report as the final word without testing it against the policy.
2. Arguing before the factual record and insurer position are clear.
3. Allowing insurer relationship concerns to weaken client advocacy.
4. Failing to maintain a chronology that another professional can inherit.
5. Closing the claim without feeding lessons into the renewal.

A closed claim should teach the renewal. What control failed? Which wording worked as intended? Which sublimit proved inadequate? Did the insurer's service match the expectation used at placement? Was the deductible economically sensible? Did the client preserve evidence properly? Could the loss have been prevented or reduced?

This is where claims experience becomes risk intelligence. The broker who closes the file and forgets it wastes some of the most expensive information the client will ever generate.

> *A claim does not need theatre. It needs evidence, coverage reasoning, persistence and a professional who remains calm when the client cannot afford to.*

PART FOUR

THE PROFESSION UNDER PRESSURE

Ethics, regulation and technology are changing what competent broking requires.

CHAPTER EIGHTEEN

Ethics, Compliance and the Invisible Lines

Ethics becomes interesting only when there is something to lose. It is easy to declare that the client comes first when the insurer, broker and client all want the same outcome. The professional test arrives when remuneration, relationship, urgency or internal pressure points in a different direction.

18.1 The conflicts that actually occur

Brokerage creates structural conflicts because the client depends on advice while much of the broker's remuneration may be paid by the insurer. The existence of that model does not make advice compromised. Pretending the conflict does not exist is what creates the danger.

The practical disciplines are familiar but demanding: disclose relevant remuneration and relationships where required, document why a recommendation serves the client's needs, avoid steering business because a market relationship is commercially convenient, and ensure that incentives inside the brokerage do not quietly reward behaviour the compliance manual prohibits.

18.2 The UAE's current standard

The CBUAE Insurance Brokers' Regulation effective in February 2025 states the point more clearly than older regional practice did. Brokers and their staff must act honestly, fairly and transparently and act in the client's best interests when comparing insurance products, rates, conditions and insurers. Recommendations must be consistent with the client's demands and needs.

The same regulation also changed money movement. For primary insurance, clients pay premiums directly to insurers. Brokers may not collect those premiums, claim settlements or premium refunds. That rule removes one category of operational risk but creates a different responsibility: the broker must communicate the process clearly, maintain evidence, reconcile accurately and ensure that coverage is not assumed merely because a client thinks payment has been made.

18.3 Compliance is a design problem

AML, sanctions, data protection and conduct controls are often presented to staff as obligations added to the real work. That framing is one reason controls fail. A control that requires a busy employee to remember an exceptional step at the end of a process will eventually be missed. The better question is how the workflow itself can make the right action easier and the wrong action harder.

That lesson became very practical for me during the CBUAE targeted financial sanctions examination of our brokerage. The examination did not ask whether experienced people knew what sanctions screening meant. It asked whether the institution had a documented risk assessment, a specific risk appetite, controlled screening thresholds, mandatory data fields and evidence that the process operated as intended. We closed the findings, but the more lasting lesson was cultural: 'we know what to do' is not the same as 'the organisation can prove what it does.'

18.4 Saudi enforcement and the regional direction

The same direction is visible in Saudi Arabia. In February 2026 the Insurance Authority said it had identified more than 2,000 violations during 2025 across supervisory, cybersecurity, customer-protection and AML/CFT requirements, with financial penalties of roughly SAR 25 million and product suspensions in some cases. Enforcement makes abstract rules real very quickly.

18.5 A professional boundary I would not trade

In every long career there are moments when the commercially convenient answer is not the professional answer. Sometimes it is a client asking you to omit a fact because 'the insurer did not ask.' Sometimes it is pressure to place with a market that pays better. Sometimes it is an internal request to treat a payment as received before the evidence is there. These moments rarely arrive labelled as ethical dilemmas. They arrive labelled urgent.

My rule is simple: if I would be uncomfortable explaining the decision later to the client, the board and the regulator in the same room, I should not make it now.

18.6 Conflicts of interest are ordinary, not exceptional

A broker is paid within a market of commercial relationships. Insurer remuneration, volume arrangements, referral relationships, sub-broking, related parties and sales incentives can all create conflicts or the appearance of them. The professional response is not to claim that a good person cannot be conflicted. It is to identify the conflict, manage it, disclose where required and ensure the recommendation can survive scrutiny.

The best test is uncomfortable: if the client saw the complete commercial arrangement, would the advice still look like the advice you would have given without it? If the answer is uncertain, the conflict is not theoretical.

18.7 Compliance should make good decisions easier

Poorly designed compliance creates forms that people complete after the decision. Good compliance shapes the decision while it is being made. A client mandate obtained at the start clarifies authority. A sanctions-screening workflow prevents a transaction from progressing without the right data. A needs analysis makes the reason for recommendation visible. An approval threshold stops an individual from overriding a control silently.

This is why technology and compliance increasingly converge. A rule embedded in a workflow can be stronger than a policy nobody reads, provided the rule itself is well governed and exceptions remain visible.

The danger is false comfort. A green screen is not proof that the underlying data is right. Automation can enforce a bad threshold as efficiently as a good one. Controls still require ownership, testing and judgement.

CHAPTER NINETEEN

Technology, Data and the Broker Who Still Matters

Technology is no longer a chapter about the future of broking. It is about the operating environment of broking now. Quotations arrive through portals. Claims move through digital workflows. Medical approvals are algorithmic. Insurers use automated fraud controls. Brokers increasingly extract data from documents, compare market responses, generate reports and monitor renewals with systems that did not exist a decade ago.

The wrong question is whether technology will replace brokers. Some broking work should be replaced. Re-keying the same policy data into several systems is not a profession. Manually reconciling insurer statements line by line is not where human judgement creates value. The important question is what work should be automated so that professionals have more time for the decisions that actually require them.

19.1 What I learned building technology inside a brokerage

When we began developing our own digital operating platform, the first instinct was naturally to automate visible friction: document intake, comparison, reconciliation, reporting and workflow. The more important lesson arrived later. Every automation creates an authority question.

If a system extracts a vehicle detail from a document, who confirms it before the quotation goes out? If a matching engine says an insurer payment corresponds to a particular transaction, at what confidence level can finance post it automatically? If a recommendation engine ranks insurers, can an adviser see why? If a binding workflow is triggered, what prevents a false 'accounted' status when the underlying journal entry has failed?

Those are not coding questions. They are broking and control questions expressed through technology.

In our own development work we deliberately kept approval gates around consequential actions. Reconciliation logic can compare multiple insurer statement formats and assign confidence, but finance still needs a controlled approval path. Motor quote automation can extract information and build a comparison, but the adviser remains responsible for the recommendation and binding decision. That design choice slows some workflows. I consider the friction worthwhile because the alternative is to automate accountability away with the administration.

19.2 Data changes the broker's value proposition

A broker with good data can move the client conversation from anecdote to evidence. Claims trends can reveal whether a medical renewal problem is frequency, severity, network behaviour or benefit design. Fleet data can show where claims cluster by vehicle type or driver profile. Property schedules can be checked for valuation drift. Commission and receipt data can reveal operational leakage. None of these capabilities makes relationship or judgement less important. They make weak judgement easier to expose and strong judgement easier to support.

19.3 Artificial intelligence and the next boundary

Generative AI has accelerated the change because it operates in the medium insurance uses most: language. It can summarise policies, draft correspondence, extract proposal information and help analyse large document sets. Used well, it is a powerful assistant. Used without verification, it can produce professional-sounding error at scale.

The rule I use is proportionate to consequence. Drafting an internal note deserves a different level of review from explaining coverage to a client. Extracting data from a motor registration card is different from deciding that a claim is not covered. The closer technology moves to a decision affecting money, rights or coverage, the more explicit the human authority should become.

19.4 What will still matter

Market access will become easier to digitise. Comparison will become faster. Administration will continue to automate. The broker's defensible value will therefore move toward risk interpretation, programme design, negotiation, claims advocacy, governance, complex communication and trust.

That is good news for professionals who actually practise those things. It is uncomfortable news for business models that have confused distribution with advice.

19.5 The broker's data advantage is permissioned context

Insurers see the risks they underwrite. Clients see their own operations. A broker sitting across several insurers and clients can see patterns between them, but that perspective comes with confidentiality obligations. The opportunity is not to pool everything. It is to learn from information in ways that respect the purpose for which it was provided.

Claims analytics are a good example. An employer can benefit from understanding whether pharmacy, outpatient care or a small number of high-cost claims drive its medical programme. A fleet can benefit from seeing whether accidents cluster by vehicle type or driver group. A property portfolio can learn from repeated small losses. None of this requires exposing another client's confidential data.

Technology makes analysis easier. Governance determines whether it remains legitimate.

19.6 AI will remove weak work before it removes strong broking

Administrative comparison, document extraction, first-draft correspondence, data reconciliation and routine reporting are all becoming easier to automate. That should not be frightening to a profession that claims its value lies in advice. It should be clarifying.

The vulnerable work is the work that can be described as moving information from one system to another without adding judgement. The defensible work is understanding ambiguous exposure, negotiating a difficult exception, explaining a trade-off, recognising when a client has misunderstood a risk, coordinating a complex claim and being accountable for the advice.

This does not mean AI cannot affect those activities. It means technology changes what the professional needs to be good at. A broker who uses automation to create more time for judgement can become more valuable. A broker who uses it only to produce more documents faster may simply create more noise.

19.7 Build technology around decision rights

When we developed our own internal broking technology, one lesson kept returning: automation is safest when the point of human authority is explicit. A system can extract vehicle data, reconcile receipts, rank matches or prepare a comparison. The question is what it is allowed to do next.

For consequential actions, we designed approval gates and audit trails rather than treating full automation as the objective. That sometimes makes a process less impressive in a demonstration. It makes it much more defensible in operation.

The same principle applies to any brokerage buying technology from a vendor. Ask what decision the tool influences, what data it uses, who can override it, what evidence is retained, and what happens when it is wrong. Those questions matter more than whether the vendor describes the product as artificial intelligence.

PART FIVE

THE CAREER YOU BUILD

The final part is less about products and more about the professional you become.

CHAPTER TWENTY

A Career Built One Decision at a Time

A career in broking rarely unfolds according to the neat ladder shown in recruitment presentations. Mine certainly did not. There are periods when technical learning accelerates, years when relationships become the real education, accounts that change your confidence, claims that expose what you did not know, and moments when a title arrives before you feel ready for it.

What compounds over time is not seniority. It is judgement. That is why I end this book with a chapter about the professional you become rather than the position you obtain.

20.1 Apprenticeship before ambition

The first years matter because they establish habits that become difficult to change later. Learn how a policy is assembled. Read endorsements instead of relying on the comparison sheet. Sit with claims people. Ask underwriters why they declined a risk. Follow a premium from quotation to accounting. Watch what happens when a client gives incomplete information.

Young professionals are understandably impatient for client ownership. I would not discourage ambition, but I would separate responsibility from visibility. The fastest way to become genuinely valuable is to become the person senior colleagues trust with the part of the file that cannot be wrong. Accuracy is not glamorous. It is the first form of reputation.

20.2 Learn one difficult thing deeply

Breadth is useful in broking because clients do not organise their businesses by insurance department. But early breadth without depth can create confident generalists who never become technically dangerous in a good way. Pick a line that forces you to think: property and business interruption, professional indemnity, marine, medical analytics, energy, cyber, something where wording and facts genuinely interact.

Then stay with it long enough to understand why two risks that look similar on a schedule can receive very different underwriting responses. Depth teaches humility because the closer you get to a subject, the more exceptions you see. It also gives you something important in the market: credibility that is not borrowed from your employer's name.

20.3 Reputation travels ahead of you

The regional insurance market is large in premium and surprisingly small in memory. People move between insurers, brokers and clients. An underwriter you deal with as a junior may become a chief underwriting officer. A client contact may move to another group and remember exactly how you behaved during a difficult claim. Your reputation therefore travels ahead of your next business card.

I have always believed that the most useful reputation is not 'good negotiator' or 'good salesperson'. It is simpler: when this person says something about a risk, I can rely on it. That reputation takes years because it is built from ordinary files. Disclose the difficult fact. Keep the commitment. Admit the mistake quickly. Do not invent a competing quotation. Do not disappear when the claim becomes uncomfortable.

20.4 Qualifications and deliberate study

Professional qualifications matter. They create structure, expose gaps and give a common technical language to people who may have learned in very different markets. The Chartered Insurance Institute pathway remains widely recognised, and other actuarial, risk, compliance, legal and specialist qualifications may be equally valuable depending on the career being built.

But a qualification is evidence of study, not a licence to stop studying. Regulation moves. Wordings change. New technology changes process. Claims create new interpretations. I have met highly qualified professionals who could not run a difficult client meeting and experienced practitioners who stopped learning because their title became senior. The profession needs both structured education and continued curiosity.

20.5 Leadership is what happens to other people around you

Senior broking is often described in terms of revenue, portfolio size or title. Those measures are real, but they miss a harder question: do people become better professionals by working with you?

A senior broker who keeps all judgement inside their own head may be commercially successful and institutionally weak. Explain why you chose the market. Let a junior colleague sit in the claims meeting. Review the submission and explain the edit rather than simply correcting it. Share the mistake that changed your own practice. This is how professional culture survives staff turnover.

The older I become in this profession, the more I value the people who taught without making teaching feel like a favour. Their influence is still present in decisions they will never see. That, to me, is a better definition of leadership than hierarchy.

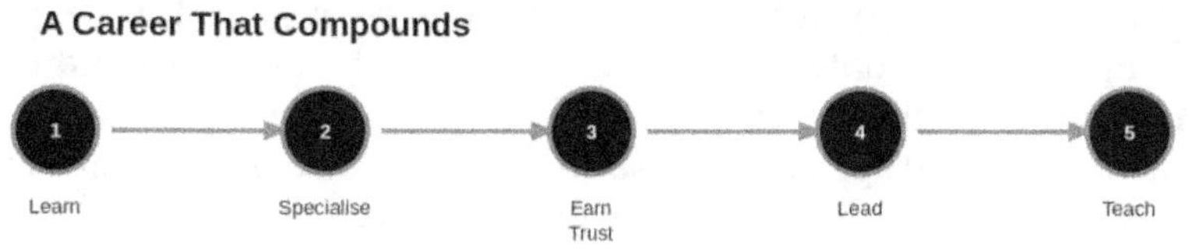

FIGURE 3 Careers compound through learning, specialisation, trust, leadership and teaching.

20.6 What I would tell a young broker now

If I were starting again today, knowing only what thirty one years in this profession have taught me, I would worry far less about titles and far more about competence. One of the great illusions of any career is believing that promotion and professional development are the same thing. They are not. Titles often arrive before judgement, and the gap eventually becomes visible. Clients can tolerate inexperience. Markets can tolerate inexperience. What neither can tolerate for very long is responsibility without capability. The best professionals I have met were rarely in a hurry. They invested time in understanding the profession properly. They learned how policies were constructed, why claims succeeded or failed, how underwriters thought, how brokers added value, and how clients actually made decisions. By the time seniority arrived, competence was already there waiting for it.

I would also encourage every young broker to become genuinely good at something difficult. Too many professionals spend years becoming broadly familiar with many subjects without ever mastering one. There is nothing wrong with breadth, but depth is what gives a professional credibility. Whether it is property and business interruption, marine, employee benefits, construction, cyber, liability, financial lines or energy, choose an area that forces you to think. Stay with it long enough to understand the nuances, the exceptions, the claims experience, the underwriting logic and the contractual detail. Over time, something interesting happens. You stop looking at policies and start understanding risk itself. That is when underwriters begin respecting your questions, clients begin trusting your judgement, and colleagues begin seeking your opinion.

I would spend much more time learning how to communicate. Insurance is a profession built on words. Policies are words. Endorsements are words. Claims arguments are words. Regulatory frameworks are words. Every day we are required to explain complexity to people who do not live inside the insurance industry. Yet some of the most technically capable professionals I have encountered struggled because they could not communicate their expertise effectively. A broker who can explain a difficult coverage issue clearly will always outperform someone who understands it but cannot articulate it. The ability to write a strong submission, a persuasive claims argument, a concise recommendation or a clear client communication is not an administrative skill. It is a commercial skill and, in many cases, a leadership skill.

I would also advise young professionals not to confuse networks with reputation. Relationships matter. They always will. Insurance has always been a relationship business. But reputation and networking are not the same thing. A network is who knows you. A reputation is what they believe about you. A network can be built quickly. A reputation takes years. It develops claim by claim, renewal by renewal, conversation by conversation and decision by decision. It is built when you disclose information honestly, when you honor commitments, when you accept responsibility for mistakes, and when you remain dependable during difficult situations. The strongest reputations are rarely accompanied by the loudest personalities. They are usually attached to professionals whose judgement others trust instinctively.

Perhaps the most important advice I would give is to teach. Most people assume teaching is something reserved for senior professionals. My experience has been the opposite. Teaching is one of the fastest ways to improve your own understanding. The moment you explain a concept to someone else, you discover whether you truly understand it yourself. Teaching exposes gaps in your knowledge, challenges assumptions and forces clarity of thought. More importantly, it transforms individual competence into professional culture. Every successful professional can identify people who invested in them early in their careers. Those contributions often have effects that last for decades. The greatest compliment a professional can receive is not simply being successful. It is knowing that others became successful because of something they learned from you.

Looking back, I realise that the most valuable opportunities in my own career rarely came from chasing success directly. They came from pursuing competence, protecting reputation, continuing to learn, and helping others along the way. The profession eventually rewards those things, even if it sometimes takes longer than we would like.

20.7 Keep a beginner's discomfort

Seniority creates a quiet professional risk: people stop telling you what you do not know. Meetings become more polite. Junior colleagues hesitate to challenge you. Familiar products feel settled. The market then changes while experience becomes a story about how things used to work.

I try to protect against that by keeping at least one area of deliberate discomfort. Read a wording in a line you do not usually place. Sit with the claims team after a difficult settlement. Ask a younger colleague to show you the technology rather than pretending you already understand it. Read the regulator's instrument instead of the market summary. The purpose is not to become a beginner again. It is to preserve the habit that made you learn in the first place.

A useful annual question is simple: what can I do now that I could not do professionally twelve months ago? If the answer is only 'manage a larger target', development has become too commercial. Growth should be visible in judgement, not just revenue.

At some point the compass stops being something another professional can hand you. It becomes your own judgement. That is the point of the profession, and the point of this book.

APPENDIX A

A PRACTITIONER'S GLOSSARY

Average clause.A provision that reduces a property claim proportionately where the insured value is below the value required by the policy basis.

Binding authority. Authority granted to an intermediary or underwriting agent to commit an insurer within defined limits.

Broker of record. The broker formally recognised as representing a client for a specified policy or programme.

Business interruption. Cover for defined financial consequences of interruption following an insured event, subject to the wording.

Capacity. The amount of risk an insurer or market is willing and able to accept.

Claims advocacy. The broker's work in helping a client notify, evidence, present and resolve a claim.

Claims made policy.A policy that responds according to when a claim is made and reported, subject to retroactive date and wording.

Cooperative insurance. The statutory structure used in Saudi Arabia for licensed insurance business.

Cover note. Temporary evidence that insurance is in force pending issue of the formal policy.

Deductible or excess. The portion of loss retained by the insured under the policy.

Delay in Start Up. Cover for defined financial loss resulting from delay to project completion after insured physical damage.

Diyya.A form of compensation associated with bodily injury or death under applicable Islamic legal frameworks; current local law must be verified.

Facultative reinsurance. Reinsurance arranged for a specific risk rather than automatically under a treaty.

Indemnity. The principle that insurance generally restores covered financial loss rather than creating gain, subject to policy and law.

Indemnity period. The maximum period for which business interruption loss is payable under the policy.

Insurable interest.A legally recognised relationship to the subject matter sufficient to support insurance under applicable law.

Loss adjuster.A claims professional appointed to investigate circumstances, coverage relevant facts and quantum.

Material fact. Information relevant to underwriting assessment; the legal disclosure test varies by jurisdiction and contract.

Placement. The process of presenting a risk, negotiating terms and securing cover.

Proximate cause. The legally relevant cause used in analysing whether a loss falls within cover, subject to applicable law.

Reinstatement basis.A property settlement basis applying repair or replacement without depreciation, subject to policy conditions.

Reinsurance. Insurance purchased by an insurer to transfer part of its own exposure.

Subrogation. The insurer's right, after indemnifying the insured, to pursue available recovery from responsible third parties.

Takaful.A Sharia compliant cooperative risk sharing model based on participant contributions and defined operator arrangements.

Underwriter. The person or function that evaluates risk and determines whether and on what terms the insurer will accept it.

APPENDIX B

REGULATORY SOURCE NOTES, CHECKED AUGUST 2026

United Arab Emirates

Central Bank of the UAE, Insurance Brokers' Regulation C 1/2024, effective 15 February 2025; CBUAE Insurance Guidelines and Rulebook; Decretal Federal Law No. 48 of 2023 Concerning the Organization of Insurance Operations.

UAE health insurance

Ministry of Human Resources and Emiratisation, Basic Health Insurance Scheme, effective from 1 January 2025 for private-sector employees and domestic workers in Sharjah, Ajman, Umm Al Quwain, Ras Al Khaimah and Fujairah; Dubai Health Authority 2025 system statistics published February 2026.

DIFC

Dubai Financial Services Authority, Insurance Supervision framework and current Rulebook, including 2026 amendments to the prudential and conduct modules.

Saudi Arabia

Insurance Authority, regulations and sector reports; transfer of health insurance responsibilities from the Council of Health Insurance effective 4 March 2024; Saudi Insurance Market Report 2024 and 2025 quarterly sector reports available on the Authority's reporting portal as checked in August 2026; Insurtech Rules, Comprehensive Motor Insurance Rules and Unified Compulsory Motor Insurance Policy.

Bahrain

Central Bank of Bahrain, Rulebook Volume 3 and Insurance Supervision Directorate materials.

Qatar

Qatar Central Bank, Insurance Supervision Department and Law No. 13 of 2012; Qatar Financial Centre Regulatory Authority for QFC entities.

Kuwait

Insurance Regulatory Unit, Law No. 125 of 2019 and implementing regulations and circulars, including 2026 market-conduct measures.

Oman

Financial Services Authority, insurance sector regulatory and legislative materials.

Jordan

Central Bank of Jordan, Insurance Supervision Department; Insurance Business Regulation Law No. 12 of 2021.

Egypt

Financial Regulatory Authority, Unified Insurance Law No. 155 of 2024 and implementing decisions.

Lebanon

Ministry of Economy and Trade, Insurance Control Commission materials and 2025-2026 sector reform announcements.

International standards

International Association of Insurance Supervisors, Insurance Core Principles; Chartered Insurance Institute professional materials; Lloyd's and major market technical guidance where relevant.

These notes identify the principal authorities used for the 2026 update. They are not exhaustive and should not be treated as a substitute for the current rulebook, legal advice or regulatory confirmation.

APPENDIX C

SELECTED SOURCES AND PROFESSIONAL READING

The book is written as a practitioner text rather than a legal treatise. The following sources anchor the regulatory, technical and professional material and provide a route for readers who want to verify or go deeper. Regulatory materials should always be checked for later amendments.

International Association of Insurance Supervisors. Insurance Core Principles and Common Framework materials. The ICPs remain the most useful international reference point for understanding how insurance supervision is expected to address licensing, governance, conduct, risk management and intermediaries.

Central Bank of the UAE. Insurance Brokers' Regulation C 1/2024, in force from 15 February 2025, together with the current CBUAE Rulebook and insurance guidance.

Dubai Financial Services Authority. DFSA Rulebook and Insurance Supervision materials for firms operating in or from the DIFC.

Insurance Authority, Saudi Arabia. Insurance regulations, market reports, customer-protection material, motor rules, health-insurance material and Insurtech Rules. The Authority began operations in November 2023 and assumed health-insurance responsibilities in March 2024.

Central Bank of Bahrain. CBB Rulebook, Volume 3: Insurance, together with current directives and supervisory publications.

Qatar Central Bank and QFC Regulatory Authority. QCB insurance instructions and Law No. 13 of 2012 for the onshore market; QFCRA rules for authorised firms in the Qatar Financial Centre.

Kuwait Insurance Regulatory Unit. Law No. 125 of 2019, implementing regulations and current decisions and circulars.

Financial Services Authority, Oman. Insurance legislation, licensing information, market reviews and supervisory publications.

Central Bank of Jordan. Insurance Business Regulation Law No. 12 of 2021 and Insurance Supervision Department material.

Financial Regulatory Authority, Egypt. Unified Insurance Law No. 155 of 2024 and the implementing decisions published by the FRA.

Ministry of Economy and Trade, Lebanon. Insurance Control Commission announcements, circulars and sector-reform measures.

UAE Ministry of Human Resources and Emiratisation. Basic Health Insurance Scheme materials concerning the extension of mandatory coverage from 1 January 2025.

Dubai Health Authority. Health-insurance system publications and annual operational statistics, including the 2025 data published in February 2026.

Chartered Insurance Institute. Core insurance, broking, claims, underwriting and legal study texts. The exact syllabus changes, but the discipline of structured professional study remains valuable.

Lloyd's Market Association and International Underwriting Association. Market wordings and clause resources, including marine and specialty-market materials. Model wordings are reference points and must be considered alongside the policy actually issued and applicable law.

Swiss Re Institute, sigma. Global and regional insurance market research, catastrophe-loss studies and protection-gap analysis.

Lloyd's. Market intelligence, emerging-risk research and technical publications relevant to complex and specialty risks.

A note on evidence

The regional cases in the main text are either drawn from the professional environment described in the source manuscript, with identifying details changed, or are expressly identified as personal practice examples from the author's own work. They are used to illuminate professional judgement, not to establish legal precedent. Where a case turns on law, regulation or a specific wording, readers should return to the primary instrument and the actual contract.

APPENDIX D

STANDARD DOCUMENTATION REFERENCE GUIDE

Standard Documentation Reference Guide

Proposal form. The client's formal application. Accuracy and completeness support underwriting and later claims.

Risk questionnaire. Extended information gathering for risks requiring detail beyond a standard proposal.

Market submission. The broker's organised presentation of risk information and requested coverage.

Indicative terms. A non binding statement of proposed coverage, premium and conditions, subject to final agreement.

Cover note. Temporary evidence of cover pending formal policy issuance.

Policy document. The insurance contract, including schedule, wording, conditions and endorsements.

Endorsement. A written amendment changing the policy terms.

Notice of loss. The initial notification of an event that may give rise to a claim.

Proof of loss. Evidence supporting cause, extent and financial quantum of the claim.

Loss adjuster report. The adjuster's findings and recommendation, which should be reviewed critically.

Broker closing. Formal confirmation of placement, participating insurers, premium and agreed terms.

APPENDIX E

SELECTED DISCUSSION QUESTIONS

Selected Discussion Questions

Chapter 1. What distinguishes professional advice from product distribution, and how would the client know the difference?

Chapter 3. How should a regional broker verify regulatory requirements when one programme spans several jurisdictions?

Chapter 4. How would you advise a client that wants to omit information which may be material but was not specifically requested?

Chapter 7. What analysis should determine a business interruption indemnity period?

Chapter 14. How would you document the reason for recommending one insurer over another?

Chapter 15. How would you deliver unwelcome advice to a senior family business decision maker without weakening the message?

Chapter 17. What should be included in a disciplined challenge to an adjuster's report?

Chapter 18. How should a broker address an incentive or remuneration arrangement that may influence a recommendation?

Chapter 20. What should a three year professional development plan contain beyond qualifications?

EPILOGUE

WHEN THE COMPASS BECOMES YOURS

A professional guide can shorten the distance between ignorance and competence. It can explain principles, introduce products, provide frameworks and point people in the right direction. What it cannot do is shorten the distance between competence and judgement. That distance has to be travelled personally. It is travelled through work, through experience, through disappointment, through mistakes, through difficult conversations and occasionally through uncomfortable truths that no textbook can properly teach.

Over the course of your career, you will participate in transactions and claims that remain in your memory long after the premium figures have been forgotten. You will sit in meetings where a single sentence buried deep within a policy wording suddenly becomes more important than every presentation, every negotiation and every technical discussion that came before it. You will discover that risks that looked simple on paper become far more complicated when they are tested by reality. You will encounter clients who challenge your judgement, underwriters who change the way you think, and situations that force you to decide what kind of professional you truly are.

You will also make mistakes.

I certainly did.

Some were technical mistakes. Others were judgement mistakes. Some came from moving too quickly. Others came from not asking one additional question when I should have. Looking back, I realise that many of the lessons that shaped me came from situations I would never have chosen for myself. At the time they felt like setbacks. Years later, they became some of the most valuable parts of my professional education.

If there is one piece of advice I would offer, it is not to be afraid of mistakes. Be afraid of refusing to learn from them. Every significant error should leave behind something useful: a better process, a better question, a stronger habit, a more disciplined approach. The goal is not perfection. The goal is improvement.

When I entered the profession, the market looked very different from the one we work in today. Entire product classes have emerged. Regulation has matured dramatically. Technology has transformed workflows that once consumed enormous amounts of time. Artificial intelligence is now entering conversations that would have sounded like science fiction when I started my career. Clients are more informed, regulators are more demanding, and expectations are higher than ever before.

Yet despite all of those changes, the profession itself remains built upon remarkably simple foundations.

Clients still need someone who can understand their business.

They still need someone who can translate uncertainty into understandable risk.

They still need someone who can distinguish a cheap answer from a good answer.

They still need someone who can read the wording, ask the difficult question, challenge the assumption, negotiate the terms and stand beside them when a loss occurs.

That part has never changed.

What technology will eventually replace are the parts of broking that never truly represented its value in the first place. Administration will continue to become more automated. Comparisons will become faster. Documentation will become easier. Information will become more accessible. None of these developments reduce the value of good judgement. If anything, they increase it. In a world where information becomes abundant, judgement becomes more important because someone must still decide what matters, what does not, and what should be done next.

After more than thirty years in this profession, I have come to believe that the most valuable asset any broker possesses is not technical knowledge. It is not market access. It is not negotiation skill. *It is trust.*

Clients trust us with uncertainty.

Insurers trust us with information.

Regulators trust us with responsibility.

Colleagues trust us with leadership.

That trust is earned slowly and lost quickly. Every file either strengthens it or weakens it. Every recommendation either reinforces credibility or diminishes it. Every decision contributes something to the professional reputation that follows us throughout our careers.

The older I become, the less interested I am in success measured only by numbers. Premiums matter. Revenue matters. Growth matters. But what stays with me most are the people. The clients who placed enormous trust in my advice. The colleagues who shared their experience generously. The mentors who corrected me when I needed it. The younger professionals who later became leaders themselves.

Those are the things that endure.

Eventually a point arrives in every career when people stop giving you directions as often as they once did. The profession stops providing clear answers and starts expecting judgement. You find yourself relying less on what somebody else told you and more on what experience, principles and perspective suggest is right.

That is the moment when the compass changes.

At the beginning of your career, someone hands you a compass.

A mentor. A colleague. A teacher. A manager. A qualification. A book.

Something helps you find your direction.

Years later, the compass becomes your own.

The real challenge then is not whether you can follow it.

The real challenge is whether you can trust it when the answers are unclear, whether you can recalibrate it when circumstances change, and whether you can use it to help others find their own direction.

Because every profession survives through people who are willing to pass knowledge forward.

One day, whether you realise it or not, someone will look to you for guidance in the same way you once looked to others.

When that day comes, I hope you will remember that knowledge is important, experience is valuable, expertise is necessary, but judgement is what ultimately gives all of them meaning.

Carry the compass until you no longer need it.

Then hand it to someone else.

Dr. Ibrahim H. Karam
Dubai, United Arab Emirates

www.ingramcontent.com/pod-product-compliance
Lightning Source LLC
LaVergne TN
LVHW050825061126
851857LV00012B/986
* 9 7 8 9 6 9 9 5 9 7 7 2 5 *